Y0-CBG-670

KNOWING
GOD'S
SECRETS

KNOWING GOD'S SECRETS

Updated Edition

JOHN HUNTER

Foreword by Major W. Ian Thomas

Fresh Springs Publications
Kingsport, Tennessee

Unless otherwise indicated, the Scripture quotations in this book are from the *New King James Version*. Copyright © 1979, 1980, 1982, Thomas Nelson, Inc.

Scripture quotations marked (AMP) are taken from *The Amplified Bible, Old Testament*. Copyright © 1965, 1987 by The Zondervan Corporation. *The Amplified New Testament*, copyright © 1954, 1958, 1987 by The Lockman Foundation. Used by permission.

The original painting on the cover was done by William Bledsoe. The unusual light shining on the path in the painting depicts the truth of John 8:12: "I am the light of the world. He who follows Me shall not walk in darkness, but have the light of life." Without the light, we could not see the secret path.

Reproductions of this painting can be obtained by writing:
William Bledsoe
P. O. Box 252
Jonesborough, Tennessee 37659

KNOWING GOD'S SECRETS

Copyright © 1965 by Zondervan Publishing House
Copyright © renewed 1995 by Fresh Springs, Inc.
Kingsport, Tennessee 37664

ISBN 1-886797-02-1

All rights reserved. No portion of this book may be reproduced in any form without the written permission of the Publisher.

Printed in the United States of America.

Have you heard the counsel of God?
Do you limit wisdom to yourself?
(Job 15:8)

The secret of the LORD is with those who fear Him . . .
(Psalm 25:14)

CONTENTS

FOREWORD

As a speaker some years ago at a convention in the South of England, I was at once struck by the forthright manner in which the Chairman handled the proceedings. I determined then and there to get to know something more about him.

Thus it was that I first came to know John Hunter, at that time Headmaster of a school at Wiltshire. The invitation which brought him to our Conference Grounds at Capernwray Hall as Guest Speaker eighteen months later was the next link in that chain of events which has so amply justified those early impressions.

John Hunter came to the North of England as Headmaster of a Christian School in a neighboring town, so that he might more fully participate in the many-sided activities of the Capernwray Missionary Fellowship of Torchbearers. As Founder and General Director, I knew a particular joy when he accepted the invitation to join the preaching staff of the Fellowship. The years that have passed since then have served only to deepen my affection for him and for his family, and to enhance my respect for him as a man of God whose ministry became richer with every added responsibility.

It is sad indeed that there are so many true and earnest believers who think of a victorious Christian life as a "super deluxe" version, instead of normality, and in the words of the author, are "so busy enduring their failure that they have no time to enjoy their faith." The message of this book is designed to demonstrate to all its readers in terms that all can understand, that the mystery of how to "be" what as Christians we have been born-again to "become" is now an open secret in Jesus Christ—that the secret of a *changed* life is an *exchanged* life!

No need now "to shuffle on through life—despondent and downhearted," for it is the happy lot of every child of God to step out confidently into the daily adventure of proving that our "future tense" is gloriously secure in the settled certainty of a timeless God Who knows the end from the beginning, and that we never need to "go" without knowing that we have been "sent."

I am confident that all who have the privilege of reading the following pages will discover spiritual principles to which they will be able to return again and again, and always find them true—principles by which the simplest and the humblest may enter into the very secrets of God.

—Major W. Ian Thomas

1

The Barrenness Of Ignorance

When your car won't start, or when it suddenly fails you just when you need it most, it is good to know how to put it right. What a relief to be able to lift the hood, adjust a nut, fix a faulty connection, and then feel the engine surge back to life. Just a little "know-how" can make all the difference. It can save you money, it can save you time—it could even save a life.

When someone in your home is ill, especially if that someone is your child, it is good to know what to do. It is reassuring to recognize the symptoms, remember what you have done on previous occasions, and act accordingly.

In the same way, when failure and weakness come into your experience, when tragedy strikes and circumstances threaten to engulf the little world of "me and mine," it is good to know what to do. It is reassuring to have an answer which is more than a platitude.

But do we? Do we actually have the answer in our possession?

In 1 Corinthians 2:12, we are told that "we have received, not the spirit of the world, but the Spirit who is from God, that we might know the things that have been freely given to us by God." Or to put it simply, *we have received in order that we might know.* The tragedy of many Christians is that although they have received, they do not know. They have been saved, converted, born again—whatever expression you use—but they do not possess that quality of knowledge which interprets human experience in the light of divine truth. They do not have the "know-how."

By continuing in Jesus' word I can know truth. It is the application of truth that makes me free—not the mere acquisition of it.

This knowledge was promised to us by Jesus. His words to those who believed on Him are recorded in John 8:31-32: "If you abide in My word, you are My disciples indeed. And you shall know the truth, and the truth shall make you free." Notice that the promise was given to those who had believed. By continuing in Jesus' word, I can know truth. It is the *application* of truth that makes me free—not the mere *acquisition* of it. In John 8, the Lord Jesus was speaking of a future experience, because the work of redemption was not yet accomplished and, as a result, the Holy Spirit had not yet been given. But in 1 Corinthians 2, the experience set forth is both available and in operation today. It is not "we have received so that, some day in the future, we shall know", but "we have received . . . that we might know," here and now.

When I was a young Christian, I often heard wonderful messages preached on 1 Corinthians 2:9: "Eye has not seen, nor ear heard, nor have entered into the heart of man, the things which God has prepared for those who love Him." The preachers would turn our eyes away from the "wilderness journey" and its sorrows and frustrations, and paint for us in glowing colors the glory that would be ours in the next world. "Yes," they would say, "eye has not seen, nor ear heard. We have no idea what a blessed prospect awaits us. God has prepared it all for us!" We were encouraged to put up with our miseries, to accept failure as the normal Christian life, and to keep looking ahead. The promise was always, "Someday it will be yours."

Now while it is true that in the coming world there is nothing but blessing, this is not the truth taught in 1 Corinthians 2:9-10. *"The truth shall make you free,"* said the Lord Jesus, but that kind of preaching produces no freedom; it only makes the chains more comfortable. The preachers forgot to do what the Lord instructed. He said, *"if you continue in my word."* But they didn't continue; they stopped at the end of verse 9. If they had continued into verse 10, they would have discovered that all the promises of verse 9, all the things which God has prepared for those who love Him, are ours *now.* "God has revealed them to us through His Spirit." We do not have to wait for them or pray for them; we can appropriate them and enjoy them here and now. So the Christian life is no longer waiting for the blessing to come "in the sweet bye and bye," but appropriating the power and the joy hour-by-hour, moment-by-moment.

There is thus all the vast potential of blessing unknown to the heart of man, waiting to be revealed by the Spirit, and "we have received . . . the Spirit who is from God, that we might know the things that have been freely given to us by God." The Christian life becomes a treasure hunt, a possessing of possessions, a daily unfolding of the things freely given by God.

But it is this quality of Christian living which is unknown to so many of God's people. They face situations and problems to which they have no answer. They accept defeat and barrenness as the normal Christian experience. They are not equipped to glorify God in the midst of tragedy. As a result they have no joy, no peace, no freedom, and no comfort to share with others.

Many of God's people accept defeat and barrenness as the normal Christian experience. They are not equipped to glorify God in the midst of tragedy.

I have been preaching and teaching the truths of God's Word for many years in conferences, colleges, and churches. I have spent hours engaged in individual counseling, talking to young, old, and older about the problems in their lives. I have listened to stories of tragedy and disaster, to the accounts of broken hearts and broken homes. Nearly every one to whom I have listened was a true Christian, born again and saved by the blood of Christ—but they were all living in 1 Corinthians 2:9. The only hope they could see was the peace of the world to come.

Now while this is very sad and pathetic, we should realize that such Christians are dishonoring to God and to Christ. Their testimony to the world around is to the effect that God doesn't have the answer to the world's problems. They are so busy enduring their failure that they have no time to enjoy their faith. The one thing the world needs to see today is a quality of joy that cannot be obtained by human logic.

Paul's letter to the Philippians was written in prison, but it is the most joyous book in the Bible. Seventeen times in four short chapters the word joy or rejoice appears. Verse 4 of chapter 4 has rung out over the centuries: "Rejoice in the Lord always. Again I will say, rejoice!"

Rejoicing is not a hilarious giggle or a crazy uncontrollable laughter. It is the result of the application of truth. It is the glowing experience of freedom, a consciousness of the absence of burdens, an unusual sense of being uplifted in spite of pressures and circumstances around.

The purpose of this book is to take truth and apply it to our hearts. We will examine some of the things that are freely given to us by God so that, by His Holy Spirit, what is revealed may become reality in our experience.

Two things need to be understood before we dig into the treasury of truth. The first is that these things are already *freely given to us of God.* Since they are already given, God doesn't have to give them to us again. Because they are already given, we don't have to spend days or weeks or years asking for them. We have just to take what God has already given, and say "thank You."

Do you remember what happened when you first trusted Christ and accepted Him as your own personal Savior? For most of us, the day came in our spiritual experience when we saw ourselves as sinners in the sight of a Holy God. We recognized our position, and we looked for a Savior. We heard from the Gospel that "God so loved the world that He gave His only begotten Son, that whoever believes in Him should not perish but have everlasting life." Somehow we recognized that this was for us. By the power of God's Holy Spirit, we came to see that we had to make a decision. There was no need for us to keep on asking or to keep on waiting. We had simply to receive the gift that God had offered.

I remember what a blessing it was when I read John 1:10-14, to see especially in verses 11 and 12 that although Jesus "came to His own, and His own did not receive Him," yet to "as many as received Him, to them He gave the right to become the children of God, to those who believe in His name." I had always looked upon believing as a mental process whereby I agreed with what was said. It was something that happened in my head. But here I discovered that "believing is receiving" and "receiving is believing." I found out that when I really believed on Jesus, I had actually received Him into my life. I didn't understand it, but I knew I wanted Him, and so in simple faith I received Him into my heart and life. I had to learn in a very childlike way that you don't ask for a gift that is being offered to you. You just receive it and say thank you!

So we will need to keep on remembering as we read these truths that these things are already *freely given to us by God*. We need to prepare our hearts not to be continually asking for what God has already given. As His Holy Spirit reveals the truths in His Word and we see our barrenness and emptiness, we must learn with childlike trust that faith is the empty hand outstretched to receive what God is already offering.

The second thing we need to understand as we go into these studies is that we have received God's Spirit *that we might know*. The emphasis here is on *knowing*. This is not a matter of speculation, or trial and error, but a definite positive act of knowing. In a world loaded with uncertainty and bewildered by doubt, the true Christian is the only one who can take a stand and say, "I know."

This was the transcendent courage of Paul as he wrote 2 Timothy. Humanly speaking, Paul's life was a failure. He had lost everything that men of his day and age and class counted valuable and vital. He was

---

In a world loaded with uncertainty and bewildered by doubt, the true Christian is the only one who can take a stand and say, "I know."

---

expecting any day to complete his tragedy of degradation by losing his life. But there was a quality of experience filling his heart which enabled him to cry out from the condemned cell, "I am not ashamed, for I know whom I have believed" (2 Timothy 1:12). He had that positive certainty—*I know*—so dynamic that it lit up the few remaining days of his life with a glory that has reached down across the years.

This glorious confidence is the birthright of every true Christian. God has no favorites. What He did for Paul, He can do for us today, if we will take of the things so freely given to us by Him.

God receives no glory when His children are caught up in the panic of a mad world, when the fears and frustrations that invade every area of a godless humanity find their insidious way into the lives of His own people. The fears are present, and the tragedies do exist—it would be foolish to deny this. But the Christian who is equipped with the provision of God has an answer to the sorrow and sordidness of life.

> *God receives no glory when His children are caught up in the panic of a mad world, when the fears and frustrations that invade every area of a godless humanity find their insidious way into the lives of His own people.*

This confidence of knowing is evident in every line of Psalm 23. Verse 4 says, "Yea, though I walk through the valley of the shadow of death, I will fear no evil." Notice there is no walking *around* the valley of the shadow of death. There is no avoidance of the testing, but there *is* a glorious confidence—*"I will fear no evil."* This is not so in many Christians' lives today. So many of God's people do not have the confidence which says, "I know—I am not ashamed—I will not fear!" And yet the Word of God is very clear. *We have received . . . that we may know.*

This indwelling confidence is not for the favored few. It is not a quality of Christian experience which should be called "the victorious Christian life" or "the deeper life." This is the normal Christian life as taught in the Word of God; anything else is subnormal. Our ready acceptance of such phrases as "the victorious Christian life" is a libel on God and upon His plans and promises. In one sense, it suggests that the defeated life is the normal life, that when we become Christians we have to accept a shoddy inferior Christian experience as God's accepted pattern. The tendency is to offer the "victorious Christian life" as a super-deluxe version, only achieved by selected super-saints, and only after an acceptable time of apprenticeship.

If we do this, we fail to see that whatever God offers is always perfection. Every sunset is always perfect, every snowflake is absolutely exquisite, every bird's egg is a marvel, every baby is a miracle. James 1:17 says that "every good gift and every perfect gift is from above, and comes down from the Father of lights, with whom there is no variation or shadow of turning." The gifts are always good, always perfect.

If God's gifts are always perfect, especially the gift of the Christian experience, then why do so many of God's people live in the shadow of fear and produce lives so uninviting to the world around, and so uninspiring for the Church? The answer is surely that we have never taken all that God is prepared to give. And because we have never taken, we have never possessed; and because we have never possessed, we have never been able to say "I know Whom I have believed."

Many of us are able to say "I know *what* I have believed." We can look back to an experience or to a situation which brought us into the Christian faith. But the older we grow, the further we move from that crisis of experience. The unfolding tragedy is that the increasing years often take us away from that which brought us so much joy and peace. If my experience is linked only with *what* I have believed, then I will never know the thrilling daily wonder of knowing *Whom* I have believed.

It is possible to be tremendously busy in many Christian activities, to be linked up with fine groups and organizations, and yet to have an inward experience of barrenness and dryness. In Romans 10:1-2, Paul records his impassioned prayer to God for Israel: "For I bear them witness that they have a zeal for God, but not according to knowledge." The Jewish people had enthusiasm without enlightenment—and enthusiasm alone is not enough. I have met Christian workers and pastors who have been very zealous for God. Judging by the amount of personal interest and effort involved, they were very busy about their Master's business. But in spite of all their enthusiasm, they had an inward emptiness of soul and a deep longing for an experience with God that would bring peace to their anxious hearts. They, too, had a zeal for God, but not according to knowledge.

Truly the barrenness of ignorance is one of the greatest tragedies in the Christian Church today. The fruitfulness of faith is God's answer. This is our aim as we read this book together.

2

The Secret Of Being A Saint

We have already considered the words of the Lord Jesus in John 8:31, "You shall know the truth, and the truth shall make you free." Notice again the important fact that it is the *application* of truth that sets me free, not the *acquiring* of truth. There are many true Christians whose knowledge of doctrine is correct in every detail. They can spot the mistakes in the sermon and they can correct the flaws in the argument, but they do not have a present enjoyment of the truths they know in their heads. Because of this, there is something missing in their lives. Some unknown deficiency shows itself in their daily experience. As a result, they themselves are disappointed both in their daily experience and in their outside interests. Somehow, they have never found the secret of being a saint.

Some people are just naturally gracious and pleasant in their ways. But when we consider the secret of being a saint, we are moving into an experience which goes far beyond mere pleasantness. Many of us would dearly love to be more saintly in our ways and behavior so that we could attract more people to the Lord, but so often we write ourselves off as a dead loss. We accept our temper and meanness as hereditary. We satisfy the prickings of conscience by looking back and seeing the same characteristics in our parents and our grandparents.

I have sometimes seen a child with his nose pressed against the window of a brightly decorated store, gazing at things that could never be his. They were so near and yet so far. I have sometimes met Christians who, in like manner, have their spiritual noses pressed against the "window" of a joyous, successful, and blessed spiritual community. They, too, were seeing things that would never be theirs—Christians who were calm, rejoicing in adversity, who had an inward glowing peace, who had overcome great sorrow and tragedy. Those outside just gazed in hungry envy—so near and yet so far. They had accepted their lack of saintliness as their natural lot.

Such Christians look at the characters in the Bible and seek for one with whom they can identify themselves. This is one reason why Peter is such a popular personality. We read of his mistakes and his reactions, and we feel a sense of kinship. We are attracted to Peter because we see ourselves in his failures.

On the other hand, there are some characters who seem so holy and saintly that we almost tiptoe past them in case we disarrange their holiness. Such a man is the Apostle John, "the disciple whom Jesus loved." To many Christians, the man John is the ultimate in godliness. "If ever a man was a saint, it was the Apostle John," some would say. They think of his lovely writings in the gospel, the epistles, and Revelation, and they have an immediate image of one who was the epitome of peace, love, grace, and quiet dependability.

If this is true, John can teach us little about the secret of being a saint—because he must have been born a saint in the human sense. However, when we turn to the Word of God, we find some very interesting situations in which John was involved.

Mark 3:13-19 gives the account of Christ's choosing and ordaining His followers. Twelve names are listed, but the first three are specifically pin-pointed. Peter, James, and John were given surnames

---

The Lord Jesus called John "the soon angry one." What a nickname to give to a young man!

---

or special names by Jesus, names that indicated their personality. It is worth noting that it was *Jesus* who called them by these names, not the other disciples—they might have used something stronger! Simon He surnamed Peter, the rock, but the two brothers James and John He surnamed Boanerges. The New King James Version reads, "He gave the name Boanerges, that is, 'Sons of Thunder.'" This translation—the Sons of Thunder—is ambiguous and conveys no definite meaning. A more literal translation gives Boanerges as, "the sons of rage," "the soon angry ones"—quite a different proposition. The Lord Jesus called John "the soon angry one." What a surname or nickname to give to a young man! And it was Jesus who gave it. What kind of a personality must this young man John have had to be called such a name by the Lord Himself? This is not the name to give to a saintly character.

Doctor Luke gives us several insights into the life and mind of John, especially in chapter 9. Jesus wanted to teach His disciples humility (verse 47). To illustrate His teaching, He used a visual aid: He called a child to come and sit by Him. Jesus continued to teach words of truth (verse 48).

But suddenly (verse 49), John breaks into the quiet teaching with the words, "Master, we saw someone casting out demons in Your name; and we forbade him because he does not follow with us." What an amazing situation! Christ was teaching humility, and suddenly John bursts into the middle of the message. Luke says that "John answered." Notice that nobody had asked John anything. He was the kind of person who gave answers to questions nobody ever asked. His interruption showed that he had not listened to what the Master had said. He had been thinking of what he had done, and he suddenly burst out and boasted of it. This was the very *opposite* of humility, both in what he said and how he said it.

Later on in verse 51, we are told that Jesus, "when the time had come for Him to be received up, that He steadfastly set His face to go to Jerusalem." This journey took Him through Samaria. When night came, a search was made for lodgings for thirteen men. When the request for accommodation was made, the Samaritans refused, point blank, to receive them. This does not indicate that the Samaritans were being unusually unpleasant—they were just being Samaritans. John 4:9 tells us "for Jews have no dealings with Samaritans," and the Samaritans were simply responding in a similar way.

Luke 9:54 gives us the reaction of James and John to this refusal: "when His disciples James and John saw this, they said, 'Lord, do you want us to command fire to come down from heaven and consume them, just as Elijah did?'" They meant every word they said. Here were "thunder and lightning" in action—quite prepared to blast innocent women and children into a lost eternity in order to satisfy their own rage. What kind of men would do such things? Surely not the "saintly" John, whom so many people respect and admire!

Notice the response of Christ to these words: "He turned and rebuked them, and said, 'You do not know what manner of spirit you are of.'" This word "rebuke" is a strong word. Jesus rebuked Peter once, as recorded in Mark 8:33. He also rebuked the wind (Mark 4:39). But this word is used mainly of Christ's dealing with demons and unclean spirits. It was this kind of sharp rebuke that Jesus gave to the two men who did not know what manner of spirit was in them.

On their way to Jerusalem for the last time, Jesus gave His disciples a most graphic account of what lay ahead for Him (Mark 10:33-34):

"Behold, we are going up to Jerusalem, and the Son of man will be betrayed to the chief priests and to the scribes; and they will condemn Him to death and deliver Him to the Gentiles; and they will mock Him, and scourge Him, and spit on Him, and kill Him. And the third day He will rise again."

Notice how intense this language is. See that verse 33 and 34 are all one sentence, spoken in the same outburst of intensity, indicating the pressures under which the words came forth.

We would expect that such a powerful utterance would have compelled attention, but verse 35 indicates otherwise. James and John came to Him

almost immediately after the words of Christ about
His death. The object of their coming indicates that
they had never listened to the words spoken. Christ
had outlined His program of suffering, but they were
busy with their plans for success. There is almost an
air of conspiracy as these two brothers come with this
opening request: "Teacher, we want You to do for us
whatever we ask." Notice the emphasis on the *we* and
us.

It was then that their plans became apparent. They
were expecting the Lord Jesus to go to Jerusalem and,
by His mighty power, overthrow the Roman rule and
establish His own Kingdom. When this had been
accomplished, Jesus would need strong men to help
rule His Kingdom. Here were two volunteers, seeking
for favors in the new government, for positions of high
office where they could exercise their love of power
and authority. What kind of man would go behind the
backs of the other disciples to seek favor for himself?
This is certainly not the behavior of one who was
"sweet and saintly." No wonder that "when the ten
heard it, they began to be greatly displeased with
James and John" (verse 41). The words *greatly displeased* speak of indignation and disgust. John was
certainly not a popular character at that moment.

This is the kind of personality John possessed as a
young man among the disciples. He was very far from
being a saint. He was quick-tempered, ambitious,
unlovable, and difficult to get along with.

"But," someone will say, "wasn't he the disciple
whom Jesus loved?" Yes, he was. This is how John
chooses to describe himself in his own gospel. But this
does not necessarily indicate that he was lovable. In
fact, it could indicate the opposite. Think of any large

family you know. On whom does the mother bestow her greatest love? On the best child? No, she pours out her greatest love on the most difficult one. Such an awkward child requires so much more loving and forgiving and tender care. So it was with Jesus and John.

Having pointed out these characteristics in John, we must be quick to realize also that he had one tremendous redeeming feature—he loved the Lord Jesus more than all else. His love for Christ took him to the cross of Christ. When all the others had fled and were in hiding, John was there with Mary. It was to John that Jesus committed His mother, that he might care for her. It was to Mary that Jesus committed John also, that she might be a mother to him. Jesus wanted someone to care for John personally after the crucifixion, and He chose His own mother to watch over this young man.

One might ask, from where does this general impression of John's goodness and gentleness arise? The answer is that this is the picture we find in his writings. The gospel of John and his epistles breathe out love and grace and mercy. But these were written about A.D. 90-95, when John was an old man, nearly ninety. Much had happened by that time.

But even in the Book of Acts there is a marked change. John is seen there on several occasions, but his voice is never recorded. Something had happened to John to change him from the man he was in the gospels to the man we see in the writings. In his gospel he never mentions his own name. When it was necessary, he called himself "the disciple whom Jesus loved." The picture is completely different. The hasty temper has gone, the pushing personality has vanished. Instead of being the object of "much displeasure," John is now the object of much love and respect. John had found the secret of being a saint.

Many Christians today need to find that same secret for themselves. There are still many Christians with quick tempers or pushing personalities, who constantly cause embarrassment and displeasure to their fellow Christians. Not only so, but they cause sorrow to themselves as they constantly do the things they hate so much. They realize how poor their witness is before a watching world, but they have no answer to their problem. They have never found the secret of being a saint.

Yet this secret is there for all to see in God's Word. When I became a true Christian, I repented of my sin and received the Lord Jesus as my own personal Savior. I opened my heart's door and invited Him to come in and cleanse me from my sin. On the basis of His promise in Revelation 3:20, I heard His voice and opened the door, and I know He came in.

2 Corinthians 13:5 underlines this very point: "Examine yourselves as to whether you are in the faith. Test yourselves. Do you not know yourselves, that Jesus Christ is in you?—unless indeed you are disqualified." This is the test of whether I am in the faith. I can be a church member without being in the faith. The reality of my faith is that Jesus Christ is in me. If He isn't, then I am a reprobate—a fake, a counterfeit. If Jesus Christ is in me, how does He live in Me? The Bible tells me that He lives in me in the Person of His Holy Spirit. Romans 8:9 says, "Now if anyone does not have the Spirit of Christ, he is not His." The Holy Spirit is the Spirit of Christ. That is the way He chooses to dwell in me. Galatians 4:6 says

that "because you are sons, God has sent forth the Spirit of His Son into your hearts."

As a result, I have the Lord Jesus in my heart in the Person of His Holy Spirit. There are now two powers present in my life as a Christian. There is my own personality with its own plans and purposes, and there is the Spirit of Christ. It is at this point that the secret of being a saint really becomes clear. If I want to be a Christian with a true, lovely character, then I must

---

Here is the basic rule: the secret of a changed life is an exchanged life. John became a Christlike man because he found the secret.

---

know and experience a real change of heart. But there is only one way that this can be realized. Here is the basic rule: the secret of a changed life is an exchanged life. Paul could say in Philippians 1:21, "For me, to live is Christ." There had been an experience of the exchanged life in the life of Paul, just as there had been in the life of the Apostle John. John became a Christlike man because he had found the secret also. Christ was living in John in such a wonderful way that men would see only Christ, and not the turbulent angry John.

This is such a wonderful example to contemplate, because it brings to us new hope in our daily living. If John had been born sweet and saintly we would find no encouragement in his story, but rather a standard which condemned us without giving us the hope of escaping from it. But John wasn't always sweet and saintly; he was like so many Christians today—awkward, unlovely, quick-tempered, and difficult to get along with. John's willingness to know a changed life through an exchanged life brings to each of us today the challenge to open our hearts and lives to the over-ruling presence and power of the indwelling Spirit of Christ.

We began this chapter with the words in John 8:31, "You shall know the truth, and the truth shall make you free." What we have considered in this chapter is truth. The knowledge of this truth alone will only bring us frustration, and this is the position of many Christians with whom I counsel each year. They know the truth, but for some strange reason they hesitate to apply it to their own hearts and lives. Rather than yielding their lives to the full sway of Christ, allowing Him to dictate the policies and the purposes of their lives, they shuffle on through life. Sometimes they are in disgust, other times in despair. They become despondent and downhearted because they never become dependent on Christ for everything.

This, then, is God's secret for being a saint—the exchanged life. What we do about it is our responsibility.

3

The Secret Of Behaving Like A Saint

Many of the people with whom I counsel are real Christians who have come to a spiritual crisis. They have trusted Christ as their own personal Savior, and they are in real earnest about loving Him and serving Him. They are not content with "just being forgiven." They have a desire for a deeper life, a closer walk, a life of dedication, and an experience of "the victorious life." In order to obtain this blessed experience, they have faithfully followed all the instructions they could hear or read. Some have yielded their lives to Christ many times. Others have dedicated their whole beings to His service repeatedly. Many have said, "I have yielded my life, I have laid my all on the altar, I have dedicated all I am and have—but still I have no sense of completeness in my soul. I still feel I'm missing something, somehow, somewhere."

This experience can be most disheartening and frustrating to the sincere Christian. Some, as a result of this frustration, turn their eyes inward upon themselves, and search for sins or situations which might be holding back the blessing. But, having searched and confessed, they still find themselves in a position of weakness and failure. Their beliefs are correct, but their behavior falls short of what they had anticipated.

They have learned the secret of *being* a saint, but they have never found the secret of *behaving* like a saint. To their sorrow, they have discovered that being a saint is not the same as behaving like a saint. They are not content to be what they are, but they have not found the secret of being what they know they should be.

Many sincere Christians have discovered, to their sorrow, that being a saint is not the same as behaving like a saint.

We can find help in this problem when we turn to John's first epistle. This first epistle is most important, for it is God's last letter to us, written about A.D. 94. It is called the General Epistle, since the other two are for specific individuals. It contains no new church truth or doctrine, but it is a personal application of truth to the heart and life of the individual believer.

In John's writings as a whole, and especially in the epistles, the key word is *love*—God's love. This word *love* is a translation of the Greek word *agape´*, one of the least common words in classical Greek. It expresses only the highest and noblest form of love. It is not so much an emotional response as a characteristic attribute. It means the "givingness" of the one who expresses love. It is interesting to see how often in the Scriptures this love is linked with "givingness." John 3:16 is the supreme example: *"For God so loved the world, that He gave His only begotten Son."* James 1:17 tells us, "Every good gift and every perfect gift is from above, and comes down from the Father of lights."

All that we ever possess and experience in the Christian life is the result of the "givingness" of God. The complimentary action to giving is taking—not asking. My personal experience of God's love in my heart is the measure in which I respond to the "givingness" of God. When I came as a sinner and realized that God was offering forgiveness, I took this gift so freely offered. Because I took, I enjoyed the blessings

> *This is one of the basic truths of the Christian faith: God is offering all that I need in every area of Christian experience.*

of forgiveness of sins. I had peace with God through our Lord Jesus Christ. We see the same idea in the gospel stories where Christ so often said to a healed person, "your faith has saved you." We know that the source of the healing was in the Person of Christ, but the actual experience only came when the seeker took, or appropriated, for himself the blessing so freely available.

This is one of the basic truths of the Christian faith: God is offering all that I need in every area of Christian experience. Not only is God giving that which makes me a Christian; He is also giving, moment-by-moment and hour-by-hour, that which enables me to live the Christian life. Ignorance of this fact is the cause of the failure we are considering in this chapter—failure to understand the secret of behaving like a saint.

1 John 4:7-21 is a wonderful section dealing with the love of God. The word *love* is used twenty-seven times in these fifteen verses.

Verse 10 says, "In this is love, not that we loved God, but that He loved us, and sent His Son to be the propitiation for our sins." Here the love of God is concerned with "the act of Christ"—He came to be the propitiation for our sins. This is the Cross-work of Jesus. We find the same thought in Isaiah 53:5: "But He was wounded for our transgressions, He was bruised for our iniquities; the chastisement for our peace was upon Him, and by His stripes we are healed."

In 1 John 2:2 the same word "propitiation" is used, meaning "that which appeases": "And He Himself is the propitiation for our sins, and not for ours only but also for the whole world." Notice the tense in which this is written—He *is*. It is present tense, showing us the continual efficiency of the blood of Christ to deal with the question of sin. Of this we read in Hebrews 9:24: "For Christ has not entered the holy places made with hands, which are the copies of the true, but into heaven itself, now to appear in the presence of God for us."

Even today the death of Christ is the one and only answer for the question of sin and sins—and all this is the outcome of the love of God.

Verse 9 of 1 John 4 reads thus: "In this the love of God was manifested toward us, that God has sent His only begotten Son into the world, that we might live through Him." There was a time when I used to think that verses nine and ten were saying the same thing. But a closer examination revealed that these two verses were presenting two different facets of truth concerning the person and work of Jesus Christ. Both are the outcome of the love of God, but each is vitally necessary to a successful Christian life. Verse 10 is concerned with dying, but verse 9 is concerned with living—"that we might *live* through Him." In verse 10 we read of Jesus paying the price for our sins. I am the sinner, and therefore I should die; but Jesus is the propitiation for my sins. Because He died for me, I am dead in Him. No more will a holy God ask payment for my sin; when Christ died, I died in the sight of God. So the teaching of verse 10 is *that I might die through Him.*

Verse 9 on the other hand is dealing with an experience whereby I might *live through Him,* moment-by-moment and hour-by-hour. Notice how the love of God was manifested to produce this glorious experience—*God sent His only begotten Son into the world.* It is the sending of the only begotten Son that opens up for me the possibility of living through Him.

Paul taught a similar truth when he was preaching in Antioch in Pisidia. The story is told in Acts 13:14-33. Paul was preaching to both Jews and Gentiles as verse 16 makes clear: "Men of Israel, and you who fear God," as does verse 26: "Men and brethren, sons of the family of Abraham, and those among you who fear God, to you the word of this salvation has been sent." Paul's message was to Jews and Gentiles, and it concerned *the word of salvation.* Verses 32 and 33 contain tremendous teaching concerning the fulfilment of the promise of this salvation: *"God has fulfilled this . . . in that He has raised up Jesus."* Notice that Bethlehem did not fulfill the promise of salvation; it was the Resurrection of Christ that was the glorious fulfilment of God's promise. The risen Christ was God's answer to man's need.

Then Paul, led by the Holy Spirit, went on to say: "He has raised up Jesus. As it is also written in the second Psalm: 'You are My Son, Today I have begotten You.'" In an amazing way, Paul was led to teach that Psalm 2:7 was fulfilled in the Resurrection of Christ, that it was on that day of resurrection that God said, "*I have begotten You.*" We know the teaching of God's Word which states that the Lord Jesus was always the only begotten of the Father (John 1:14, 18). But here in Paul's speech, the Holy Spirit presents a facet of truth that unlocks the secret of 1 John 4:9. In a special way, Jesus was begotten in resurrection—this is the teaching of the Holy Spirit through the ministry of Paul. Jesus was born at Bethlehem, but He was begotten in resurrection.

When this key is put into the lock of 1 John 4:9, a glorious truth emerges. "In this the love of God was manifested toward us, that God has sent His only begotten Son [the risen Christ] into the world, that we might live through Him." This is the answer to the secret of behaving like a saint. I am not expected to live *for* Jesus, but God in his great love has sent the risen Christ that I might live *through* Him.

We have already seen in the previous chapter that when I became a Christian, Jesus Christ came to live in my heart in the person of His Holy Spirit. True Christianity is really "Christ-in-you-ity." It is the conscious sense of the presence of Christ that makes the real Christian life a thrilling and glorious adventure. Now, when I see this added truth, that God's wonderful love caused Him to send the risen Christ into my heart so that I might live through Him, a whole new conception of living is possible for me. I don't have to struggle to behave like a saint, to put on an act and reach a high enough standard. God doesn't expect me to imitate Christ or to live for Christ.

Jesus said in John 3:6: "That which is born of the flesh is flesh, and that which is born of the Spirit is spirit." So many Christians are struggling to make the flesh perform the works of the Spirit. This is impossible. God expects nothing of "me" but failure, because all I am is the flesh. This thought can be a tremendous relief to some poor soul who is struggling

---

I don't have to struggle to behave like a saint, to put on an act and reach a high enough standard. God doesn't expect me to imitate Christ or to live for Christ.

---

so hard to live for Jesus—you never can, and you never will. All you can do is fail and experience the sorrow that Paul had: "For what I am doing, I do not understand. For what I will to do, that I do not practice; but what I hate, that I do . . . For the good that I will to do, I do not do; but the evil I will not to do, that I practice" (Romans 7:15,19).

God wants me to avail myself of His full salvation—not only "the act of Christ" when He died for me on the cross of Calvary, but also the "activity of Christ" as He lives in my heart through His Holy Spirit. God's salvation is not a place, or an experience, but a Person—His Son. Salvation is not a crisis which begins and ends at the cross; it is both a crisis which begins at the cross and a process which continues day by day as I recognize Christ dwelling in my heart.

This is the secret of behaving like a saint—not my putting on a tremendous performance of imitating Christ, but my recognizing that God's salvation begins at the cross, and that it continues throughout my life.

We meet the same thought in 2 Peter 1:3: "As His divine power has given to us all things that pertain to life and godliness. . . ." God has already given me *all* the things—not some of them—*all* the things I need for life and godliness. In other words, if I want to behave like a saint, I have all that it takes—not in my own resources or from my own worked up enthusiasm but as a gift from God, from the *agape´* of God. *God has given me all things.* I have all things for life and godliness, for living before men and for living before God.

Salvation is not a crisis which begins and ends at the cross; it is both a crisis which begins at the cross and a process which continues day by day as I recognize Christ dwelling in my heart.

Why is it, then, that so many Christians never live in the richness of this provision? Possibly some of you who read these words are of those who "look in" from the outside—so near and yet so far. This is the blessed experience you long for but have never possessed. Consider with me how basically simple it is. It has to be simple, because it is for all ages and all times. We have already considered our God as the giver of every good and perfect gift. We have already commented on His love—His *agape´* that gave and keeps on giving. We have also seen that the complimentary action to "giving" is "taking." If God has given these precious gifts and I do not possess them or enjoy them, it is not because I haven't asked for them but because I have never taken them!

I have counseled with brokenhearted Christians who were asking and begging for peace in their hearts. How wonderful it was to be able to show them that we don't ask for a gift that is already being offered—we simply take it and say "thank You." It has been such a glorious experience to teach these dear people to take in simple faith what God has already given.

I remember one lady who had been asking and begging for peace in her heart for fifteen years. She was a true Christian, but she had realized something was missing. For many years she had longed for a quiet peace in her own soul. As we talked, I suggested that for the next three days she should not ask for a single thing. Instead, she learned how to pray in a new way—like this:

"Thank You, Heavenly Father, for so great a salvation. Thank You for the Lord Jesus who died on the cross so that my sins might be forgiven. Thank You, also, that the same Lord Jesus lives in my heart and life in the person of His Holy Spirit. Thank You, Lord Jesus, that You live in my heart. Thank You that You are my peace, You are my joy, You are my strength. You are all that I can ever need or want. You have promised never to leave me or forsake me—I believe this. Thank You for Your promises that never fail."

We prayed this way together, and then she went home with a thankful heart. I saw her each day for the rest of the week, and the change in the woman was amazing. Christ became relevant to her daily living. As she thanked Him, she drew near to Him and He drew nearer. By the end of the week, her soul was saturated with the peace of God and she was living life in a new dimension—not because she asked, but because she took and said, "thank You." Because she had inward peace, her home had peace and her family was blessed. Her husband was encouraged and her children were happy. The whole family moved out from under the shadow, just because the mother took what God was offering.

Perhaps God has been speaking to you as you have read these pages. Have you ever taken Christ as your own personal Savior? This is where you begin, at the cross, confessing your sin, repenting of it, and accepting Christ into your heart and life as your friend and Savior.

Perhaps you are a Christian bogged down with failure and frustration. Why don't you turn from this experience and come to God with empty hands, taking all that He gives for all that you need. God's answer is Christ—that you might live through Him moment-by-moment and hour-by-hour. Think of the words of Paul, one of the greatest, most successful Christians who ever lived—*"For to me to live is Christ."* His was a present tense experience of the sufficiency of One Who never fails anybody, anytime, anywhere.

4

The Secret Of Constant Joyfulness

One of the most overworked words in the English language is *love*. It is used in connection with ice cream, sunsets, scenery, symphonies, babies, and a thousand other things. A film full of lust and sins is heralded as a *love* story—and the Bible says that God is *love*. We use the same word in English, but its meaning differs tremendously.

The word *love* is the great key word in John's precious epistles, but the word used in the original is very special to the New Testament. There are four words in the Greek language which have been translated by the one word love. *Eros* is the love of a man for a woman—a passionate love. The word is never used by New Testament writers. *Philos* is the warm love for those nearest and dearest; it tells of the feelings of the heart. *Storge* is the affection expressed and enjoyed between parents and children. Finally there is *agape´*, the great Christian word used and developed in the New Testament. This word is uncommon in classical Greek; it speaks of unconquerable benevolence.

Love—*agape´* love—is not an emotion. It is the outstanding revealed characteristic of God. God *is* love (1 John 4:8). God *always* is love. He never has to work up emotion. God's love is the "givingness" of God, seen in so many Scriptures—*"God so loved the world, that He gave His only Son"* (John 3:16).

In John's three letters he uses this word *agape´* as a noun eighteen times and as a verb twenty-four times, making a total of forty-two times in one hundred eleven verses—more than once in every three verses. This remarkable emphasis carries special implications.

John's letters were written soon after A.D. 90, the last Biblical letters to be penned. Sixty years had passed since the death of Christ, and two new generations had arisen. John's writings teach no new truth, nor are they directed at promoting church discipline. But the emphasis on the word *love* reveals his awareness of the lack of love in those days. The lack is emphasized again in the Book of Revelation, written by John about A.D. 96. In chapter 2, he is writing to the church at Ephesus. Paul had written the great Ephesian letter to these Christians thirty years before—a letter full of the highest truth—but John brings them a challenge now. In verses 2 and 3 he speaks of their works, their labor, and their patience. He has much to say that is complimentary. But then he adds in verse 4, "nevertheless I have this against you, that you have left your first love."

John's method in his letters is to hold up the glory and wonder of the love of God, and then to call for a response from our hearts. This is seen so beautifully in 1 John 3:1-2: "Behold, what manner of love the Father has bestowed on us, that we should be called the children of God." John, in spite of ninety years, was still overwhelmed at the amazing miracle of the love of God. The purpose of God's love was to bring us into a relationship with Him, and the verses go on to tell us what "we should be," what "we are," and what "we shall be."

To realize the full impact of these letters we must keep on remembering to whom they were written. More than half of the population of the Roman empire were slaves. Thus many of the Christians who first heard these letters would be men and women with no rights, no possessions, and—in one sense—no personality. Historical records exist in which Roman farmers indicate the number of their four-legged cattle and of their two-legged cattle—the slaves they possessed. These despised people, who were called "things," would hear of a God who cared for them. Those who were unrecognized by their masters would realize that in Christ they had a relationship with God; they were called *the children of God*. John was calling men to a new sense of dignity by which they could rise above the chains and apathy of the slave life.

This is the whole purpose of the first chapter of John's first epistle. In the first two verses, he tells of what he had seen and heard. He was the last living link with Christ. John had seen Him, he had heard His voice, he had "handled" Christ. Now, he says in verse 3, "That which we have seen and heard we declare to you, that you also may have fellowship with us; and truly our fellowship is with the Father and with His Son Jesus Christ."

One of the outstanding glories of the Christian faith is the fellowship it inspires and promotes. John here speaks of the fellowship these Christians had with one another, and then tells forth the greatest glory of all: "truly our fellowship is with the Father and with His Son Jesus Christ." Many of these Christian nobodies would never be allowed to enter their master's home, would never be able to speak with him—they would be beneath his position and status in Roman society. But here was an amazing truth—they could have real fellowship with God the Father and with His Son. We so often miss the full impact of the honor and dignity conveyed in these words. We, as children, have the right to go directly into the presence of God. No one will keep us out.

There is a story told about the British Royal Family which illustrates this point. Many years ago, the Royal Family was visiting their home at Holyrood Palace, in Edinburgh, Scotland. The young Prince of Wales, son and heir to the throne, had somehow been out of the Palace grounds wandering about on his own. During his walk he met a boy about his own age. The boy was poorly dressed and came from a poor home, but each enjoyed the other's company. When their "adventure" was ended, the Prince took his friend "home" to meet his father. As the two youngsters approached the Palace, the sentries saluted smartly. The pair journeyed on into the Palace, passing guards and soldiers who sprang to attention as His Royal Highness approached. Finally, the young Prince came into the presence of his father, the King, and presented his new friend Tommy.

What an adventure for Tommy! He was able to walk unhindered right into the presence of the King—but only because the son of the King had made it possible.

This is our great privilege. We can go any time into the presence of the King of Kings—but only because the Son of the King has made it possible. Tommy went in his rags, but we go as sons of God, dressed in the righteousness of Christ.

So it is that John's first letter opens with the *fact* of our fellowship, recorded in verse 3. John goes on in the next verse to mention the *fruit* of our fellowship: "And these things we write to you that your joy may be full." Fullness of joy is the fruit of our fellowship—first with each other, then with the Father and with His Son.

The title of this chapter is "The Secret of Constant Joyfulness." Here is the secret from the Word of God. The fuller my fellowship is, the fuller my joy will be. Constant joyfulness is dependent upon constant fellowship. But notice, this isn't a fellowship of withdrawal from each other unto God. It begins with our fellowship with each other, which in turn promotes our fellowship with the Father and with His Son, Jesus Christ.

In dealing with young children we sometimes explain the word *joy* by taking the three letters J, O, and Y. We say J stands for *Jesus* first, O is for *others* next, and Y is for *you* last. Another explanation is to take the J, which stands for Jesus and the Y which stands for You—then to show that to have joy there must be nothing in between the J and Y.

This last illustration is basically true with regard to fullness of joy and fullness of fellowship. I can never know fullness of joy if there is something hindering my fellowship with my brothers and sisters in Christ. What I am with God depends first on what I am with others. This is shown so clearly in Matthew 5:23-24: "Therefore if you bring your gift to the altar, and there remember that your brother has something against you, leave your gift there before the altar, and go your way. First be reconciled to your brother, and then come and offer your gift." Notice that Jesus says we are to leave our sacrifice if our brother has anything against *us*—not the other way round. If I am out of fellowship with my brother, I cannot bring my gift to the altar.

Having spoken about the *fact* of our fellowship and its *fruit,* John goes on in verse 6 to speak about the *failure* of our fellowship. "If we say that we have fellowship with Him, and walk in darkness, we lie and do not practice the truth." The failure of our fellowship, and thus of our joy, is due to "walking in darkness" and not "doing" the truth. Notice that John was including himself in this possibility of failure before applying it to all true Christians—if *we* say.

The phrase "do not practice the truth" is unusual. We usually think of "speaking" the truth, rather than "doing the truth." But here John describes Christians who say and profess to have fellowship with God, but whose actions show otherwise. Truth is primarily what I am and what I do—not just what I say!

Psalm 40 has a similar thought. In verse 3 we read, "He has put a new song in my mouth—praise unto our God; many shall see it and fear, and will trust in the LORD." God has put a new song in my mouth, but it is a song that is seen, not heard! It is when the "many" see the song in my life that they fear and trust in the Lord.

All Christians are agreed that "actions speak louder than words," and that behavior must match up to belief. But there are a vast number of Christians who do not practice what they preach. One of the present tragedies in the Church is the absence of joy in so many lives. The world around is never impressed when I have all my doctrines correct in theory, but it stands open-mouthed and hungry when it sees a Christian who is demonstrating *the secret of constant joyfulness.* One joyful Christian is worth a thousand church members whose lives are as dull as the rest.

This short chapter ends with a further thought about the fullness of fellowship. All the way through this chapter John keeps on using the pronoun "we," thereby including himself in all the situations. The truth that follows on the *failure* of fellowship with one another is essential to a fuller fellowship with God.

The world around is never impressed when I have all my doctrines correct in theory, but it stands open-mouthed and hungry when it sees a Christian who is demonstrating the secret of constant joyfulness.

In verse 9, John gives us one of the greatest secrets of the Christian faith: "If we confess our sins, He is faithful and just to forgive us our sins and to cleanse us from all unrighteousness." There is one thing necessary on our part—*if we confess our sins.* There must first be the *walking in the light,* as told in verse 7, because light reveals. Those in failure walk in darkness (verse 6), so that they cannot be disturbed by the sight of their sins. But those who want fellowship and joy walk in the light. They choose to expose every situation and circumstance to the holy light of God so that their sins and failures will be revealed. Then the promise of verse 9 can be exercised and enjoyed. It is a promise of rich blessing which is conditional on our confession. If we will do one thing, God will do two things. If we confess our sins, God will forgive us and cleanse us—because He is faithful and just.

1 Peter 2:24 tells us concerning the Lord Jesus that He "Himself bore our sins in His own body on the tree." When Christ died, he died bearing my sins, paying the price of my sins. He died for me. The price has been paid, so that when I come in humility, confessing my sins, my sins are forgiven. They are forgiven because God is just. Justice was satisfied at the cross. They are forgiven in the sight of heaven because that is where the efficacy of the blood of Christ is displayed, even today. 1 John 2:2 tells us that Jesus "is the propitiation for our sins"—not "He was," but "He is." Jesus is *still* the propitiation for our sins.

We are not only forgiven our sins, but verse 9 tells us that we are *cleansed* from all unrighteousness. We are forgiven because God is just; we are cleansed because God is faithful. If we knew only that we were right in the sight of heaven, we still would not be properly equipped for successful victorious living on earth. There would still be the sense of uncleanness in relation to ourselves. Regret, shame, and sorrow could cripple us and limit our further development in God's sight and in God's service. This is where the wonder of God's provision is so precious. He not only forgives us in the sight of heaven; He also cleanses us in the sight of ourselves. He has promised that if we confess our sins, He will also cleanse us from all unrighteousness. This is the additional promise we can claim. Cleansed in the sight of God as well as forgiven, we can step out of the regret and the shame and the sorrow, and go forward once more walking by faith in the light.

The devil will come and remind us of our sins and failure. He will tell us how unworthy we are even to bear the name of Christ. With all of this we so often agree. The very memory of our failures disrupts our plans and withers away our joy, and we return to a dry, brittle, joyless life which is useless to God or man. How wonderful it is when we can claim the added promise of 1 John 1:9—not only forgiven, but cleansed. God not only forgives and forgets; He cleanses and covers with the righteousness of Christ.

The secret of constant joyfulness is keeping short accounts with God, walking humbly in the light, confessing all known revealed sin, accepting forgiveness, and claiming cleansing.

When this precious verse is taken and applied in all its fullness, then the fellowship is restored and the joy is full. "The secret of constant joyfulness" is keeping short accounts with God, walking humbly in the light, confessing all known revealed sin, accepting forgiveness, and claiming cleansing. Constant claiming and constant cleansing bring constant peace and joy.

5

The Secret Of True Friendship

True friendship is something rare and special—for several very good reasons. Many of us have friends and acquaintances who are dear to us in differing degrees, but not many of us have a quality of association with another that could be described as true friendship. True friendship requires a perfection from both the parties concerned. A one-sided friendship, where one person is responsible for the things that bind and strengthen, is never a true friendship. Jesus said to His disciples in John 15:14, "You are my friends if you do whatever I command you." These are such simple words, but if we apply them to ourselves, they break us down and make us really search our hearts. *"If you do whatever I command you"*—a tremendous challenge.

True friendship, whether between man and God or man and man, depends basically upon the type of commitment there is one to the other. For true friendship, this commitment has to be experienced and shared in a threefold way—the area of my commitment, the depth of my commitment, and the quality of that commitment.

This can be seen by examining several specific friendships mentioned in the Bible. Most of us, when we think of perfect friendships, call to mind David and

Jonathan. We remember the lovely story of the shepherd boy and the King's son. We recall David's pathetic lament in 2 Samuel 1:17-27, especially his words in verse 26, "I am distressed for you, my brother Jonathan; very pleasant you have been to me; your love to me was wonderful, surpassing the love of women." We accept this as an example of true friendship.

This friendship began in 1 Samuel 18. The exciting story of David's victory over Goliath and the resulting crushing defeat of the Philistines is recorded in chapter 17. In verse 1 of chapter 18 we read, "And it was so, when he [David] had finished speaking to Saul, the soul of Jonathan was knit to the soul of David, and Jonathan loved him as his own soul." These two young men thus began their great friendship. Right from the start it was one of tremendous emotional intensity—*he loved him as his own soul.* Verse 4 of the same chapter describes how Jonathan visibly demonstrated his love for David by giving David his robe, his sword, his bow, and his belt.

Chapter 19 begins with Saul's hatred of David and his command to all his servants, and to Jonathan, that David had to be killed. Verse 1 ends with these words, "But Jonathan, Saul's son, delighted greatly in David," and verses 4-7 tell how Jonathan spoke well of David to Saul his father (verse 4). Jonathan's defense of David was such that Saul changed his mind and revoked his command, and David was restored to his position of favor and leadership.

Chapter 20 is the next section in the story of this great friendship. David was again under the wrath of Saul, and he appealed to Jonathan for assistance. "So Jonathan said to David, 'Whatever you yourself desire, I will do it for you'" (verse 4). In verses 16-17 Jonathan made a covenant with David. We read that "Jonathan again caused David to vow, because he loved him as he loved his own soul." Verses 41-42 describe how the two separated: "They kissed one another; and they wept together, but David more so."

Chapter 23 gives the last recorded meeting between them. In this chapter David is being hunted by Saul, but "Jonathan . . . arose and went to David in the woods and strengthened his hand in God. And he said to him, 'Do not fear, for the hand of Saul my father shall not find you. You shall be king over Israel, and I shall be next to you. Even my father Saul knows that" (verses 16-17).

These are all the accounts we have of the friendship. But although they express deep love and devotion, there is something missing, especially when the friendship is examined as an experience of true commitment in every area, in penetrating depth, and in challenging quality.

Basically, this was a friendship that failed—because Jonathan was not fully committed to David. It was highly emotional but never very practical from Jonathan's side. There is an important incident recorded in 1 Samuel 18:4: "And Jonathan took off the robe that was on him and gave it to David, with his armor, even to his sword and his bow and his belt." Here Jonathan gave David his robe, which denoted his rank as the King's son. Then he gave him his weapons, and finally his belt, which contained the purse in which he carried his money and his riches. So Jonathan gave to David his rank, his resistance, and his riches.

But there was one very important item of personal equipment he did not share—his shoes. To us, the shoe is just an ordinary item of footwear. But in the days of the Bible, a man's shoes were much more than ordinary footwear. There are instances where a man was commanded to take the shoes from off his feet because the place where he was standing was holy. In the story of the prodigal son, when he returned to his home, his father commanded the servants, "Bring out the best robe, and put it on him, and put a ring on his hand and sandals on his feet" (Luke 15:22). Without the shoes, he was a servant; with the shoes, he was a son.

Then in Ruth 4:7 we read these unusual words: "Now this was the custom in former times in Israel . . . to confirm anything: one man took off his sandal (shoe), and gave it to the other, and this was a confirmation in Israel." The giving of the shoe was the clinching of the deal, a proof that the business was settled in the sight of all the onlookers. But Jonathan did not give his shoes, though he gave all else. That which would have made their covenant legally binding and practical, he never performed.

If we check Jonathan's subsequent behavior, we find that every time he went out to speak with David, he always went back to his own home and left David as an outcast. In 1 Samuel 20:42, Jonathan spoke very lovely words of comfort and peace, but David "arose and departed, and Jonathan went into the city." Later on we read that "David stayed in the woods, and Jonathan went to his own house" (23:18). Jonathan is always shown as going back—in the shoes he didn't commit! He felt for David and he fought for David, but he never followed David.

In 1 Samuel 22:1-2, we have the wonderful story of the Cave of Adullam and of the way in which people joined David there. "So when his brothers and all his father's house heard it, they went down there to him. And everyone who was in distress, everyone who was in debt, and everyone who was discontented gathered to him. So he became captain over them."

But Jonathan never joined them.

That which would have made their covenant legally binding and practical, Jonathan never performed.

These men who followed David became his mighty army. There are many brave deeds recorded concerning them. Some of them risked their lives for David. Some of them even died for him. All of them followed him with utter devotion and sincerity, but Jonathan wasn't there. These men are not remembered for the words they said, but for the deeds they did. There are no emotional speeches of love recorded from these men, but their friendship with David was absolute and complete because their lives were committed to him—in every area, in penetrating depth, in challenging quality.

Jonathan was never fully identified with David. When David moved off into the pathway God was directing, Jonathan was never with him. He never committed his will to David. 1 Samuel 23:17 shows us that Jonathan had made his own plans for the future. He went back to his palace, to his plans—and he went back to perish. If Jonathan had followed David, he need not have died.

This story can come as a real challenge to us. How far are we committed to the Lord Jesus, and to what depth? Many of us use words expressing our deep love and devotion. We sing hymns and choruses with fervor and enthusiasm—"Oh, how I love Him, how I adore Him!" But true friendship with Christ is more than words: "you are My friends if you do whatever I command you," Jesus said. "If you *do*," not "If you *say*." Like Jonathan, we are prepared to give to the Lord only so much. But the deciding factor is not how much we give, but what we keep back. We, too, can keep our "shoes"—our own will—and as a result, our friendship with Jesus Christ is limited and our effectiveness is minimized.

Many of us use words expressing our deep love and devotion to the Lord Jesus. But true friendship with Christ is more than words.

Another example of a friendship that failed, but which was afterwards restored, is the association Peter had with the Lord Jesus. In Matthew 16:13 Jesus asked His disciples, "Who do men say that I, the Son of Man, am?" Several answers were given. Then the Lord asked, "But who do you say that I am?" Peter then gave his wonderful answer: "You are the Christ, the Son of the living God." Through the inspiration and revelation of God, Peter was enabled to proclaim this glorious truth and thus identify himself with the Person of Christ.

When we look further down the same chapter to verse 21, we find that the Lord began to outline to His followers the events of His coming suffering. In plain simple words He gave them the program that lay ahead. Verse 22 goes on: "Then Peter took Him aside and began to rebuke Him, saying, 'Far be it from You, Lord; this shall not happen to You.'" What an amazing scene! Peter actually laid his hands on Jesus, turned Him around, and openly rebuked Him. In a strange misuse of language, he called Jesus "Lord," but contradicted all He had said.

Peter was committed to the Person of Christ, but not to His program. Like Jonathan, he had his own ideas as to what should happen. How true this is of most of us. We too can speak up boldly on the deity of Christ and call Him "Lord." But when it comes to

---

Peter was committed to the Person of Christ, but not to His program. Like Jonathan, he had his own ideas as to what should happen.

---

this program of suffering and rejection, we rebel. We, too, are committed to the Person of Christ, but not to His program.

Just before the events in the Garden of Gethsemane, the Lord Jesus again outlined the program for that fatal night: "All of you will be made to stumble because of Me this night, for it is written: 'I will strike the Shepherd, and the sheep of the flock will be scattered" (Matthew 26:31). Once again Peter's voice was heard. This time, he did not deny the events foretold by Christ, but he was emphatic in his determination to stand by his Master, whatever happened. Peter had his own ideas: "Even if all are made to stumble because of You, I will never be made to stumble." Peter was promising personal support, but the Lord took him up on that very point. "Assuredly, I say to you that this night, before the rooster crows, you will deny Me three times." The others were only going to desert Jesus, but Peter was going to deny Him. Proud Peter refused to take this denunciation and replied, "Even if I have to die with You, I will not deny You!" Peter had his own plans. He was going to be sufficient to handle the whole situation, even to the point of dying!

Each of the four gospels records Peter's attack on Malchus later that night in the Garden of Gethsemane (John 18:10). Peter tried to work out his own plan—but it all failed. The completeness of his failure is also recorded in every gospel, as he denied his Lord and Master.

Luke 22:54-62 shows the gradual collapse of Peter's promises and his plans. In verse 54 we read that "Peter followed at a distance." He was still following Christ, but only in his own strength, and he was *at a distance*. Verse 55 records how Peter went into the hall of the high priest's house. Here the enemies of Jesus kindled a fire, and as they sat around to warm themselves, "Peter sat among them." He wasn't following Jesus now; he was identified with Jesus' enemies.

Then came his threefold denial (Luke 22:56-60). So wrapped up was he in his own schemes and their failure that he completely forgot the words of Christ "you will deny me three times." Mark 14:71 gives the painful fact that "he began to curse and to swear, 'I do not know this Man of whom you speak!'" Not only was Peter now denying the program of Christ, he was denying His very person. The whole miserable tragedy culminates in Luke 22:61: "And the Lord turned and looked at Peter. Then Peter remembered . . . So Peter went out and wept bitterly."

Here was a friendship that failed, even as Jonathan's failed, because Peter's will was not committed to Christ. The Bible records two men going out in deep emotion following the capture of Christ. One was Peter, who wept bitterly; the other was Judas Iscariot, who went and hanged himself. The difference between these two men was that Judas never made any recorded commitment to Christ at all. Peter tried and failed, but Judas never was the friend of Christ. Judas never called Jesus "Lord." The word he used was *Master* or *Teacher* (compare Matthew 26:25, 49).

But if Peter's friendship for Christ failed, the Lord was utterly true to Peter. The Bible records how eager the Lord Jesus was to meet Peter on that glorious resurrection morning. It was as if the Lord, in His understanding of Peter's broken heart, wished to let him know that there was still love and forgiveness available for him. Mark 16:7 records how the angel at the empty tomb said to the women, "But go, tell His disciples—and Peter. . . ." There was a special message for Peter. In 1 Corinthians 15:3-8 Paul, writing of the reality of the Resurrection, said that Christ, "was buried, and that He rose again . . . and that He was seen of Cephas, then by the twelve." This is the only indication we have that the Lord Jesus made a special personal appearance to Peter. We are not told where it was, when it was, or what was said, but it does indicate the love of Christ for Peter. Shining through the tears of the broken Peter came the precious forgiving love of Jesus. Peter had failed, but his failure wasn't final.

John 21:15-19 tells the lovely story of how this friendship was restored. There is a dramatic quality about the way in which the Lord Jesus prepared the setting for Peter's reinstatement. Peter and several others had been out fishing, when John recognized Jesus because of their miraculous catch of fish. "Then as soon as they had come to land, they saw a fire of coals there" (verse 9). This was most unusual, since the normal thing would be a fire of wood. But this was a fire of charcoal. If we check back to John 18:18, we find that when Peter denied Christ it was beside *a fire of coals*. A charcoal fire has a definite pungent smell. How this would bring it all back to Peter's mind—the fire, the smell of glowing charcoal, and the Lord! Then, just as Peter had made his boasting before the disciples in the Upper Room, so now the Lord dealt with him before the same men. Three times Peter had denied his Lord, so three times that same Lord challenged his love and commitment.

Each time the Lord addressed Peter, He called him "Simon, son of Jonah." This must have hurt Peter. When he first met Christ, the Lord said to him "You are Simon the son of Jonah. You shall be called Cephas"—or Peter, the rock (John 1:42). *You are . . . you shall be* were the words then. But now the Lord Jesus takes Peter right back to the beginning again. No longer was he the rock, but the ordinary old Simon.

In His first question (verse 15), the Lord asked Peter, "Do you love me more than these?" Peter had said that "even if all are made to stumble because of You, I will never be made to stumble." (Matthew 26:33). He had boasted that he loved Jesus more than the others. Now he was challenged on that point. The word the Lord used in His question "Do you love Me?" denotes the highest quality of love and devotion. But when Peter replied, "You know that I love You," the word he used for *love* was different from the one used by Christ. Peter implied that he had a great affection for Christ, not the highest quality of love and devotion.

Verse 16 records how the Lord asked Peter the second time, "Do you love Me?", still using the word denoting the highest quality of love, but now not comparing Peter's love with the devotion of the others. The Lord, as it were, reduced His standard of measurement. First it was "more than these?" Now it is just "do you love Me?" Peter's reply was the same—he professed an affection for Christ.

"He said to him the third time, 'Simon, son of Jonah, do you love Me?' Peter was grieved because He said to him the third time, 'Do you love Me?" (verse 17). Peter might well be grieved and upset. When the Lord asked him the third time, "Do you love Me?", He lowered His standard yet further: He used Peter's own word for love. Jesus said, "Do you really have any affection for me?" Peter once more professed that he had an affection for his Lord.

To each of Peter's replies the Lord answered, not by dismissing his love, but by giving him a job to do. First it was, "Feed My lambs" (verse 15), then "Feed My sheep" (verse 16-17). The last direct word the Lord Jesus said to Peter is recorded in verse 19: "when He had spoken this, He said to him, 'Follow me.'"

Jesus took Peter right back to the beginning and gave him a new start. Peter began all over again, following his perfect Friend. This was the one thing Jonathan never did—he never followed David. Gone were Peter's plans for his own future now. He heard the Lord Jesus tell him His program for his future: "'when you are old, you will stretch out your hands, and another will gird you and carry you where you do not wish.' This He spoke, signifying by what death he would glorify God" (verses 18-19). There was no rebuke or rebellion from Peter this time. His silence showed his commitment was complete.

6

The Secret Of Facing Every Situation

One of the greatest texts of the Christian faith is Philippians 4:13: "I can do all things through Christ who strengthens me." This was Paul's great cry of defiance to a world that closed in on him from every side.

As we have seen, the epistle to the Philippians is a most blessed letter which has brought strong encouragement to God's people through the ages. It demonstrates Paul's capacity to live above his circumstances through a strength that was not his own.

It should be a challenging thought to us today to consider what sort of letters we would write if we were in prison, with no real charge against us, but with no real hope of regaining our freedom. We would have every ground for complaint, every reason to grumble and moan about how we were suffering for the Lord's sake. How strange it is to read these words of Paul in Philippians, and to see the way he rode above the complaints. Far from being a tragic picture of injured spiritual innocence, he emerges as a joyous victor. Instead of making his letter a rousing call for special prayer support in his tragic imprisonment, he uses the letter to build up and encourage the faith of those to whom he was writing. Paul had a secret which was in full operation, a secret which turned seeming tragedy into glorious triumph. Paul was able to handle these prison circumstances so that they produced for him a quality of Christian experience which far surpassed that of most of his readers—to whatever age they belong. It is this secret we hope to look into in this chapter.

The Amplified Bible has an excellent way of opening up the inner meaning of the Scriptures. It digs below the surface and reveals for us a crispness of thought we might otherwise have overlooked. This is especially so in Philippians 4:11-13. Verse 11 begins, "Not that I am implying that I was in any personal want, for I have learned how to be content (satisfied to the point where I am not disturbed or disquieted) in whatever state I am."

Verse 12 drives home this quality of contentedness: "I know how to be abased *and* live humbly in straightened circumstances, and I know also how to enjoy plenty *and* live in abundance. I have learned in any and all circumstances, the secret of facing every situation. . . ."

Notice how tremendous is this claim of Paul. He claims to know how to enjoy poverty and—what is often more difficult—how to handle material prosperity so that it produces complete satisfaction. Then he makes the astounding claim that he has learned the secret of facing every situation, in any and all circumstances. Paul is here demonstrating a quality of faith for which the world today is hungry. Not only the non-Christian world, but many sincere believers would give much to be able to say in all honesty that they, too, have learned the secret of facing every situation. One of the sorrows of counseling with Christians is to meet people who have all the answers doctrinally, but who cannot face the practical problems of daily living and daily suffering.

It will repay us to examine Paul's claim a little closer, to see the depth of his experience, and to understand how this man who lived nineteen hundred years ago can still speak to us today with authority and assurance.

One of the sorrows of counseling with Christians is to meet people who have all the answers doctrinally, but who cannot face the practical problems of daily living and daily suffering.

In 2 Corinthians 11:23-33, Paul introduces into his letter some personal experiences to prove his point. These experiences are written down in quick succession without any attempt to press home the sufferings involved. They represent an almost casual catalogue of catastrophe. But if we stop a moment in each verse to look a little deeper, and line up each experience against his claim—*"I have learned in any and all circumstances the secret of facing every situation"*—we soon discover that Paul, of all people, had earned the right to speak.

"From the Jews five times I received forty stripes minus one" (verse 24). This verse was written so casually, but it embraces a world of suffering. Thirty-nine stripes was the ultimate in Jewish punishment at that time. The Jews were not allowed to put anyone to death. (Christ was brought before Pilate in order to get Roman sanction for the death sentence.) But this punishment of thirty-nine stripes could, of itself, lead to crippling, blindness, and even death. The victim was stripped and helpless to protect himself against the accumulated agony of the thirty-nine strokes. The whip had several tails, each of which was loaded along its length with metal inserts. At each stroke the metal inserts would bite deep into the naked flesh, producing multiple wounds. Paul suffered this vicious punishment *five times*, receiving in all one hundred ninety-five lashes. It is amazing that his body could take such treatment. His back must have been permanently marked with scars. But the point to remember here is not the intensity of the suffering, but the success of the secret—Paul had learned the secret of facing that situation.

"Three times I was beaten with rods" (verse 25). Here the injury was inflicted on the spine, as the executioner beat the victim's back with solid unyielding rods. We know today what agony can result from spinal injury, and what further complications often show themselves in later years. Paul's suffering from the strokes of the rods, on a back already lacerated, could have laid the ground for much future agony. But in all this, he had a blessed secret that enabled him to emerge triumphant.

In this same verse, Paul bundles together eight major experiences without making a complete sentence. "Once I was stoned." This is recorded in Acts 14:19-20. There is a miracle here which is often overlooked. Paul was stoned until the people of Lystra were sure he was dead. Having convinced themselves of his death, they dragged his broken body out of the city. But verse 20 records how, as the disciples stood round his body, Paul stood up, came back into the city, and the next day walked to Derbe—a distance of many miles. Truly he had the secret of facing that situation.

"Three times I was shipwrecked" (verse 25). This is an interesting statement because we know of only one shipwreck, recorded in Acts 27. There must have been two other unrecorded incidents, one of which involved Paul's spending a day and a night drifting in the sea as a survivor clinging to wreckage. But here again, in every moment of every circumstance, Paul had the secret of facing it all.

Verse 26 is crammed with a list of eight different kinds of perils which Paul had experienced, all involving physical danger and hardship. But in verse 27 he moves from the hardness of personal, physical suffering to the more subtle agony of physical and mental exhaustion.

"In weariness and toil, in sleeplessness often." The word "sleeplessness" here indicates sleepless nights, possibly because of the weariness and pain. Notice that this came "often." Paul speaks next of "hunger and thirst, in fastings often, in cold and nakedness." Notice again the use of the word "often" applied to his being without food.

These few personal references are sufficient to underline for us the fact that Paul really knew what it was to suffer in spirit, in soul, and in body. In an age that was characterized by brutality and suffering, Paul stands high in the list of those qualified to speak from bitter experience.

The blessing to our hearts is to see that this is the man who can teach us the secret of facing every situation. He speaks from a full experience and his words are full of hope and victory.

Paul goes on to say in Philippians 4:13 (AMP): "I have strength for all things in Christ Who empowers me [I am ready for anything and equal to anything through Him Who infuses inner strength into me; I am self-sufficient in Christ's sufficiency]."

Many Christians can quote verses saying that Christ is their strength, but they cannot show a life which demonstrates the reality of what they believe.

Here then is Paul's secret, set down for all to see. The secret is based on his relationship to the risen Christ. He has strength for all things, as we have seen, but it is a strength that comes from Christ Who empowers him.

Now there are many Christians who know, in theory, that Christ is their strength. They can quote verses illustrating this fact, but they cannot show a life which demonstrates the reality of what they believe. Paul touches the vital secret when he says, "I am ready for anything and equal to anything through Him Who infuses inner strength into me." The clue is that *Christ infuses inner strength into me.*

The word "infuse" is an interesting word, especially in its other uses. We talk of infusing tea. By this we mean that into plain boiling water, tea is introduced. The mixing of the tea-leaves with the water is called infusing the tea. Once it was just plain water, but through the action of infusing it becomes tea. The water changes its color and taste. It becomes, to all intents and purposes, a different thing—because of the infusing. We can take this idea and use it to understand what it means that *Christ infuses inner strength into me.* It isn't that Christ becomes my example, or my pattern, or that He is one to whom I look upward. By the action of infusing, I become involved with Christ. There is an experience of integration whereby the Lord Jesus *becomes part of my life.*

It is good to pause here and check what we understand by the word *me*—Christ infuses inner strength into *me.* If I am not clear and definite as to what I mean by the word "me," then the process of infusing will also be loose and indefinite. I will simply be interested and enthusiastic about a matter of words.

When you look at your reflection in the mirror, you are not looking at yourself—your real self. You are looking at a reflection of the body in which you live. Likewise, when you look at your friends and relations, you are seeing, not the real friends or relations, but the body in which they are residing. The real "me" and "you" goes on forever and ever. The real "me" is my human personality, that quality of being by which my friends remember me. So it is with you. When your friends remember you or think of you, they may not conjure up a physical image of your outward appearance; they think of your personality—your kindness, gentleness, honesty—your meanness, your untrustworthiness. This "you" is based not only on your physical qualities. It is the real "you," composed of your mind, your emotions, and your will. The picture you present in these three areas adds up to form your personality.

This can be seen repeatedly in the Bible. The Biblical word for a person's inner self is *the heart*. The heart, as generally used in the Bible, does not refer to the organ which pumps the blood around the body, but to those three areas of mind, emotion, and will which make up the human personality.

In Matthew 9:4 Jesus asked, "Why do you think evil in your hearts?" In Mark 2:8, He asked, "Why do you reason about these things in your hearts?" These verses, along with many others, show that the Bible uses the word *heart* for the place where reasoning, thinking, and planning are carried on. The mind, in this sense, is part of the heart.

Matthew 18:35 speaks of forgiving "from your hearts"; Matthew 22:37 speaks of loving "with all your heart"; Luke 8:15 speaks of "a noble and good heart"—all indicating that the heart is where the emotions are found.

Mark 8:17 speaks of having a heart "hardened"; Mark 11:23 of having "a doubting heart"; in Luke 21:14 Jesus commands His disciples to "settle it in your hearts"; in Acts 11:23, the Christians are directed to continue with the Lord "with purpose of heart." These are some of the references which point to the heart as the center of the will, the place where decisions are made relating to personal response.

If we take this fact, that the human heart, the human personality, "me"—whatever word we use—is the trinity of mind, emotion, and will, then we can begin to understand a little more *the secret of facing every situation* as we consider the words of our text: "I am ready for anything and equal to anything through Him Who infuses inner strength into me." The secret is the strength, and the strength is the Savior; it is the infusing of the inner strength that makes the experience living and vital.

If Christ is going to infuse inner strength into me, it is going to be more than a brave show of words. Christ must of necessity be allowed to infuse inner strength into my mind, into my emotions, and into my will. This is a process we do not often consider or bargain for.

All of us have had an emotional response to Christ. We love Him, and we sing hymns and choruses to Him. Very often we can be deeply, emotionally moved, even to tears, so that, to those around us, we present a picture of a wonderfully loving Christian. This is often the case with young people. Teenagers, especially, can become very worked up in their emotional response to the Lord Jesus and, on the basis of this emotional surge, they can make great and wonderful promises. But, the stark, cold fact is that it just isn't enough to be emotionally moved. My emotions are essential. They play a tremendous part in providing thrust to my response, but emotions aren't everything. If my mind and my will have not become vitally involved with Christ so that He is infusing inner strength into them, then my response is unbalanced.

This three-fold design of my heart or personality is like the three-legged milking stool that was used on farms in the old days. As long as all three legs were used, the stool provided a place of perfect balance on which a heavy weight could be placed. But as soon as one of the legs was missing, the stool became utterly useless. It needed all three legs to provide stability. So it is with my involvement with Christ. Emotional enthusiasm can be tremendous and present a fine uplifting picture of a dedicated human life. But if my response is only on the basis of my emotions, then it will be completely unbalanced. Such a response is incapable of bearing the weight involved in serving Christ. This is why decisions made by Christians on the basis of an emotional upsurge just fade away. Enthusiasm is wonderful, but enthusiasm by itself is not enough!

If my response to Christ is only on the basis of my emotions, then it will be completely unbalanced. Such a response is incapable of bearing the weight involved in serving Christ.

If I mean business with Christ, then I must swing open the doors of my mind and allow Him to move in. If He is going to infuse inner strength into my mind, then He must have full authority to do what He will. 2 Corinthians 10:5 speaks of "casting down arguments and every high thing that exalts itself against the knowledge of God, bringing every thought into captivity to the obedience of Christ." This experience must begin in the human heart. Certain things may need to be cast down and cast out, high things need to be brought low, and every thought must be in obedience to Christ. If this is not so, then Christ cannot be in control; and if Christ is not in control, then He cannot infuse inner strength.

It is at this point that the reality of my emotional response is fully tested. Do I love the Lord Jesus enough to allow Him to move into the area of my mind? Will I give Him full authority to say what has to be done in this area? Will I be obedient and do what He says? If He puts His finger on certain plans or schemes or friendships and says, "These must go!", do I love Him enough to say "Yes, Lord"? Here the test of our love becomes intensely practical. Let us be perfectly honest and say that there are many Christians who deliberately choose not to be so intimately involved with Christ. They choose to follow the workings of their own desires and to exercise authority themselves. They are free to do so, but they must always remember that to have the strength and the secret of facing every situation demands a complete involvement with Christ.

If my response to Christ is to be perfectly balanced, I will need to open the door of my will and allow the Lord Jesus to exercise that power of decision which has always been mine. It is very true that the last thing we will ever give up is our will. It is even true in a wedding ceremony which begins with two separate individuals but ends with one united couple. This act of union comes about when each of the two is asked if they will voluntarily accept a position of mutual dependence; the reply is "I will." By an act of will they surrender their independence to enjoy the blessings of marriage.

So it is in my relationship to my Lord. If I really want to enjoy the full blessing of my union with Christ, then I must allow Him to be the One who will choose in the future. This is exactly the way the Lord lived in relationship with His Father—"nevertheless not as I will, but as You will" (Matthew 26:39); "I do not seek My own will but the will of the Father who sent me" (John 5:30). This is the only way for me to experience inner strength and inner satisfaction, and

to *have strength for all things in Christ who empowers me.*
There is no alternative to this trinity of commitment.
I want to do real business with God and become
involved in a personal and practical way. Religion is no
alternative to reality. Forms and ceremonies and
liturgical practices are no alternative to allowing the
Lord Jesus to perform the spiritual open-heart surgery
that all of us need.

I was counseling with a young man named Jim
several years ago. We had discussed the whole matter
of being a fully committed, involved Christian,
together with the price one had to pay to experience
this rest, this joy and peace and power. Finally, when
all the discussion was over and all the questions
answered, there was a long, long pause. Jim was
deliberating in his mind and weighing it all up. Then
he said, slowly and pointedly, "You know, it all
depends on how much I really mean business with
God!" And he was absolutely right.

7

The Secret Of Overcoming Fear

Medical science now recognizes that between sixty and ninety percent of our sicknesses are caused by emotions such as fear, sorrow, envy, resentment, and hatred. Many illnesses are peculiar to our civilization due to the strains, pressures, and speed of modern living. The increasing suicide rate seems to be an indicator of the intensity of these factors. Suicide is not found so much among the poor or the less civilized, but it increases with the advance of civilization and with the development of education. Suicide is often the ultimate response to fear—fear of the future, fear of the present, fear of being found out, fear of pressures without or within. All these add up to the final decision that there is only one way to handle this fear—to end it all.

It is interesting to turn to the Bible and find out where fear is first mentioned. Genesis 3 tells the story of the Fall of man, how man turned his back on God and chose to live in independence. Verse 8 records how the Lord God came walking in the garden in the cool of the day seeking fellowship with His creatures, but they were hiding.

"Then the Lord God called to Adam and said to him, 'Where are You?' So he said, 'I heard Your voice in the garden, and I was afraid . . . and I hid myself.'"

In this pathetic answer are the first recorded words of Adam—*"I heard . . . I was afraid . . . I hid myself."* Fear was never part of God's gift and blessing to His creatures. The Lord God had poured out His love and grace in giving to them all they needed for true joy and happiness. But independence brought fear in all its cold, chilling, gripping reality.

Fear is rampant in the world today, at every level of man's living. There are so many new nations, and each one is born into a world of fear. To all of these new nations, independence brings new fears, new pressures, and new problems. The older nations, in spite of all their confident words, look with apprehension over a world restless with immature national tensions.

> *Fear was never part of God's gift and blessing to His creatures. But independence brought fear in all its cold, chilling, gripping reality.*

Even the wonderful inventions of radio and television play their part in feeding new fuel for fear into the minds of hard-pressed humans. International and national crises are seen in minute details, and the unresolved situations become items for fear and anxiety.

Fear becomes personalized when we consider it on the domestic level and the individual level. The unceasing build-up of tragic home situations, plus the utter disillusionment pervading the hearts and minds of so many today all point to the harvest of fear that has come from those first words—*I heard . . . I was afraid . . . I hid myself.*

As I have counseled year by year in conferences and churches, I have become increasingly aware of the part played by fear in the lives of many Christians. It is as if many of them live their lives in two water-tight compartments. There is the spiritual side with all its influences of church and church associations. This side, in many cases, extends out of Sunday and into other days of the week—but it is all hermetically sealed from the rest of daily experience. Then there is the other compartment in which they live, that section which deals with earning a living, paying the bills, meeting the problems, and handling the decisions of family and future.

When these people live in the compartment of church and religion, they move into an area of escape from the world around. They become almost actors in a lovely world of spiritual make-believe. But when they move out of the sheltered corner into the hard reality of dollars and decisions, they are unprepared and unequipped to face the pressures and brutality of our modern civilization. As a result they, too, become caught up in the grip of fear which grows and extends like a poisonous weed in a beautiful garden. We have the strange paradox of Christians who sing with great feeling such hymns as:

"When peace, like a river, attendeth my way,
When sorrows like sea-billows roll;
Whatever my lot,
Thou hast taught me to say,
It is well, it is well with my soul."

Then, having sung such words of blessed assurance, they go out into a cold world of reality and join the rest of their fellow men in worrying about and fearing the very things they have dismissed in their hymns.

This reality of fear in the lives of Christians is bitterly true. It has been my sad lot to deal with the results of suicide and attempted suicide on the part of real Christians. I have listened to a Christian woman who attempted suicide, but who was saved by medical help. She was filled with a sense of shame as she spoke of the love of God and her own recent suicide attempt—but she was still in the grip of fear.

The secret of overcoming fear begins with the realization of a peculiar problem. So far in this book we have thought of "The Secret of Being a Saint," "The Secret of Behaving like a Saint" and "The Secret of Facing Every Situation." All that we have considered is absolutely true. This quality of life is real. This peace and blessedness can be ours. The Lord Jesus does live in the hearts and lives of all His redeemed people. Now follows the problem: if all this is true, then why are Christians afraid? Why do so many Christians react like the rest of their fellow men? The answer to this problem is itself the secret of overcoming fear, and that is the purpose of this present chapter.

2 Timothy is Paul's last letter. It was written under the shadow of the sentence of death, in loneliness, cold, and pain; but it breathes throughout with the spirit of confident victory. Paul writes in verse 12 of chapter 1:

"For this reason I also suffer these things; nevertheless I am not ashamed, for I know whom I have believed, and am persuaded that He is able to keep what I have committed to Him until that Day."

Here was a man who knew, in a real way, the secret of overcoming fear. He gives us a clue to this secret in these words:

"Therefore I remind you to stir up the gift of God which is in you through the laying on of my hands. For God has not given us a spirit of fear, but of power and of love and of a sound mind (1:6-7)." Paul makes no attempt to deny the fact of fear, but he does state most emphatically that *God has not given us the spirit of fear*. In other words—don't trace your fears to God.

"Every good gift and every perfect gift is from above, and comes down from the Father of lights" (James 1:17). This is our confident faith. But we need to know also what God has *not* given us—and God hasn't given us the spirit of fear. So the answer to our search for the secret of overcoming fear begins with the great discovery—we have the wrong author!

But we are still faced with the fact of fear. There is still the crowding in of problems and pressure. Christians are no more exempt from the tragedies of life than are other people. We must realize that the devil, the enemy of souls, is *always* on the move against God's people. 1 Peter 5:8-9 warns us, "Be sober, be vigilant; because your adversary the devil walks about like a roaring lion, seeking whom he may devour. Resist him, steadfast in the faith."

Paul warns us in Ephesians 6:12 that, ". . . we do not wrestle against flesh and blood, but against principalities, against powers, against the rulers of the darkness of this age, against spiritual hosts of wickedness in the heavenly places." The battle is always on. The enemy never lets up in his attacks.

The devil has no power to take away our salvation. In Colossians 1:13, speaking of our Heavenly Father, Paul says that He has "delivered us from the power of darkness and translated us into the kingdom of the Son of His love." We are forever delivered from, and translated into—but the devil hasn't called off the battle. He cannot take away our salvation, but he can take away the joy of our salvation.

One of the most effective ways of neutralizing a Christian is to take away the joy of his salvation. A joyless Christian is an ineffective Christian.

The devil is a dedicated enemy. When we were saved, he lost a subject and gained a potential enemy. If we become true soldiers of Christ, we are true enemies of the devil—and he is aware of this fact. It is *not* in his power to take us back again, but it *is* in his power to neutralize us. If he can neutralize us and make us ineffective, then he has at least cut his losses. We may be lost to him, but we are no danger to him—and in one sense, no use to God. One of the most effective ways of neutralizing a Christian is to take away the joy of his salvation. A joyless Christian is an ineffective Christian. When my joy goes, my witness goes, and when my witness has gone I am totally ineffective for God.

So it is that 2 Timothy 1:7 tells us: "God has not given us a spirit of fear." If there is fear in your heart and life, then it did not come from God. It is the devil seeking to ruin your witness by canceling out your joy.

Conversely, notice how great a witness there is when a Christian surmounts such an attack. The world is always impressed when it sees a man or a woman facing trouble and tragedy unafraid. When God is given the glory for such a victory, the witness for Christ is clear and true.

Verse 7 begins by telling us what God has not given us—*the spirit of fear*. Then it goes on to state what God has given us—*the spirit of power and of love and of a sound mind*. The Amplified Bible says it this way: "[He has given us a spirit] of power and of love and of a calm *and* well-balanced mind *and* discipline *and* self control." What a wonderful contrast to the spirit of fear—a well-balanced mind!

This leads us on to the second thought in our secret of overcoming fear. The first point was, we get the wrong author. The second point is, we get the wrong answer. The natural thing to do when faced with problems and fears is to fight them. This is the way we were taught as children. "Never give in to fear or failure. Be a man and fight against them!" We are taught to overcome our fears by fighting them, by employing all our courage and determination to resist.

All this sounds so noble and heroic—but this is exactly what the devil wants us to do. He wants us to fight him, in our own strength, for the glory of God. Once he has us involved in fighting against our fears, in trying to solve our own problems, he has us right where he wants us. None of us, by himself, is a match for the devil. Only one person has ever conquered the enemy of souls—that was the Lord Jesus Himself. The tragedy of using "the wrong answer" is that we become involved deeper and deeper in what is, inevitably, a losing battle. We may even pray more and read God's

Word more, but that is no guarantee of success. Victory is not something we win as a result of our struggles and fighting. There are many Christians who are engaged in an intense struggle for victory over sin, temptation, and fear—but they will never achieve the success they desire, because they are using the wrong methods.

1 Corinthians 15:57 is a great verse: "But thanks be to God, who gives us the victory through our Lord Jesus Christ." This is God's basic plan for victory in any and every field of Christian experience. Victory isn't something I win, but something I receive as a gift. *"Thanks be to God who gives us the victory."* In all of God's dealings with man, God is shown as giving. Man's response is always to take what God gives. Just as at the cross, as a sinner, he takes forgiveness and eternal life, so the Christian continues throughout his life, taking what God gives and saying "thank You."

So it is when it comes to the question of victory, the true Christian avails himself of what God has already provided. God *gives* us the victory through our Lord Jesus Christ. The victory is ours through our Lord Jesus Christ—not through copying Him or following Him, but simply through His person. *He is* our victory!

Colossians 2:6 teaches us: "As you have therefore received Christ Jesus the Lord, so walk in Him." My job as a Christian is to continue in the same way that I began. I began by receiving Christ as the answer to the penalty of my sins. As a sinner, I deserved eternal death because God's Word says that "the wages of sin is death" (Romans 6:23). But the Lord Jesus died in my place, as 1 Peter 2:24 says: "who Himself bore our sins in His own body on the tree." There came a day in my life when I believed this. I received the Lord

Jesus into my heart as my own personal Savior. At the same time as I received forgiveness of sins, I also received the gift of eternal life, and my name was written in heaven.

This is how I received Christ years ago. Colossians 2:6 is saying that this is to be my daily attitude: I receive all that Christ is, for all that I need. Back then, He died on the cross to save me from my sins; now He lives in my heart, in the person of His Holy Spirit, to save me *from myself.* It is the indwelling Christ who is God's answer to my fear and anxiety.

The tragedy is that so many Christians are engaged in fighting a battle which is already lost, instead of claiming a victory which is already won. So it is that Paul counsels Timothy in 2 Timothy 1:6 to "stir up the gift of God which is in you through the laying on of my hands." Paul is here referring to the Holy Spirit, who was indwelling Timothy, whom he had received

---

The tragedy is that so many Christians are engaged in fighting a battle which is already lost, instead of claiming a victory which is already won.

---

as a gift from God. Let us remember here that the Holy Spirit is the Holy Spirit of Christ, the way Jesus Christ has chosen to dwell in the hearts and lives of believers. As Romans 8:9 says, "Now if anyone does not have the Spirit of Christ, he is not His."

In 2 Timothy 1:8 Paul goes on to apply this truth to particular incidents in Timothy's experience. "Therefore do not be ashamed of the testimony of our

Lord, nor of me His prisoner, but share with me in the sufferings for the gospel according to the power of God." This is what many Christians face today, and what many Christians fear—the necessity of being identified with the testimony of Christ and with other Christians who, like Paul at that time, are not rich, important, or even socially acceptable.

Paul also encouraged Timothy to share with him the sufferings for the Gospel. Sometimes, to be a true and faithful Christian calls for these "sufferings for the gospel." I have counseled with many Christians who have faced this fear—the fear of being "out" for Christ's sake. For some who were socially important, the fear was of losing all their social friends and thereby many good business connections. This is a very real fear to a successful business man and a great test to his wife. Young adults and college men and women find this a test in their lives—the fear of being thought naive and stupid if they go all out for this "religious business."

But Paul is careful to show us how we can take this stand of not being ashamed and of sharing with him in the sufferings of the Gospel. He says (the end of verse 8) that it is *according to the power of God*. The answer to the power of the enemy as he moves in to make us afraid is *the power of God*. 1 Corinthians 1:24 presents us with the picture: "Christ the power of God and the wisdom of God." In other words, the power of God is Christ Himself dwelling in my heart through His Holy Spirit.

It is the daily and moment-by-moment application of this truth that gives me the answer to my fears. Colossians 2:6 says: "As you have therefore received . . . so walk." My Christian life is viewed here, and in many other places, as a *walk*. This emphasizes the daily continuity—walking a step at a time. It also brings all of us down to the same level, regardless of nationality, race, color, wealth, or education—because everybody walks the same way, one step at a time. Rich people do not walk ten steps at a time, and busy people do not walk a week at a time. Even the poor beggar walks one step at a time.

Colossians 2:7 tells me that if I walk receiving step-by-step all that Christ can be to me as the power and wisdom of God, then I will be "rooted and built up in Him and established in the faith . . . abounding in it with thanksgiving." Notice that I begin verse 6 by *receiving,* and I end verse 7 with *thanksgiving.* Thanksgiving is that quality of joy that blesses my witness and makes the Christian faith an attractive thing to those in search of peace and blessing. As I keep on receiving Christ, so I am rooted and built up in Him. As a result, I am established in the faith.

What a wonderful secret this is—the secret of overcoming fear. The final thing to remember is that this is the only way the Bible teaches. There is no alternative to Christ when it comes to meeting and conquering fear. As I relate my problems, frustrations, and fears to the Christ who lives in my heart, believing that He is vitally interested in my blessing, believing that He is vitally involved in the whole problem—then in the same measure I can rise above my circumstances as Paul rose above his. I, too, will be able to say with the Psalmist in Psalm 56:4,11: "Whenever I am afraid, I will trust in you. . . . In God I have put my trust; I will not be afraid. What can man do to me?"

8

The Secret of Recognizing Temptation

When I was a young Christian, recently converted and seeking to live a faithful Christian life, I was greatly distressed by the problem of temptation. The whole thing became a burden to me, and I longed to be free from the subtle agonies of failure in temptation. I used to look at older men who had been years on the way, and as I noted their quiet composure, I encouraged myself with the thought that someday my bitter temptations would disappear. I imagined that as I grew older, somehow I would assume a tangible form of holy respectability which would solve all the problems of temptation, and that I would eventually arrive at the state whereby I would be free from temptation's effects. Now that I am older, I no longer think like that. I have learned that temptation never lets up. In fact, I have learned two basic realities: first, that temptation is just as strong and subtle today as it was years ago; second, that I am basically just as weak as ever I was, just as prone to failure, just as capable of denying my Lord.

The words of the Lord Jesus in John 3:6 are just as true today: "that which is born of the flesh is flesh"—and it always will be flesh! I may work on the flesh and seek to improve it. I may educate the flesh and seek to add many social graces to its basic content. But when all is said and done, it is still the flesh, and Romans 8:8 is ever true: "So then, those who are in the flesh cannot please God."

Every one of us comes to realize this sooner or later. When we do, we are faced with three possible lines of action or reaction. We can accept the situation as it is and be content to live a life of failure and defeat. We can struggle and fight to resist, seeking to learn mental gimmicks or psychological techniques. Or we can turn to God's Word and find God's answer to this problem of temptation.

In Britain after World War II, there was a tremendous economic drive to boost and build up the export of consumer goods. Many lovely things, especially china and pottery and cloth materials, were sent abroad to help restore her financial status. The people of Britain never saw these goods—they just disappeared overseas. Occasionally it was possible to buy what was then called an "export-reject." The object wasn't good enough to be sent overseas. It was faulty somewhere in its manufacture, so it was released to the home market. The British people, starved of domestic goods for so many years, would almost fight to buy up these faulty articles. They were happy to possess an "export-reject," and they paid a high price to obtain it.

Many Christians treat their daily experience in a similar way. They are content to have an "export-reject" type of Christian life. They know it is faulty in many areas, but they assume this is all that is available for the "home-market."

We all follow the same behavior pattern in the services of our own particular church—standing or kneeling, using responses in a liturgical service or having a simple song service.

In a similar way, we so often base our Christian behavior on that of the people with whom we worship. If it is a "social" church, we develop the "social" pattern of living. If it is a "worldly" church, then standards are easier and young people grow up with a quality of Christian life almost indistinguishable from that of the world around them. Whatever type of church it is, if we are content to only live up to the standards of the majority, then we condemn ourselves to a quality of life which is unsatisfactory both in the eyes of God and in our own experience.

The Bible has much to say on the whole subject of temptation and Christian behavior. We can consider its teaching under four different headings. First, let us consider *the source* of temptation.

If we are content to only live up to the standards of the majority, then we condemn ourselves to a quality of life which is unsatisfactory both in the eyes of God and in our own experience.

In the previous chapter dealing with fear, we saw from 2 Timothy 1:7 that God has not given us the spirit of fear. Fear comes from the enemy of souls, the devil. Likewise, we learn from 1 John 2:16 that "all that is in the world—the lust of the flesh, the lust of the eyes, and the pride of life—is not of the Father, but is of the world." Just as fear is not from God, so the Bible teaches that *temptation is not from God.* James

1:13 states specifically, "Let no one say when he is tempted, 'I am tempted by God'; for God cannot be tempted by evil, nor does He Himself tempt anyone." 1 John 2:16 shows us Satan's trinity of temptation— "the lust of the flesh, the lust of the eyes, and the pride of life." We shall see in our studies that this is the devil's basic pattern of temptation. In many passages of both the Old and the New Testament, this idea is presented.

The word *lust* means "the over-desire." There are basic God-given hungers and desires built into our body and human personality. Because they are from God, they are "good and perfect gifts." Satan, in his attack on God's creatures, abuses these God-given qualities. He seeks to mold these desires into over-desires, or lusts, so that his own evil purposes can be fulfilled.

We can think of the "lust of the flesh" as a consuming passion *to do*; "the lust of the eyes" as a compelling urge *to have*; "the pride of life" as a constant thrust *to be*. This basic trinity of temptation becomes a constant dynamic *to do, to have, to be,* linked with these three desires—passions, possessions, and pride. It is remarkable, as we shall see, that this is the devil's *only* pattern of attack. All the temptations throughout the ages have come along these lines, very often in the same order given in 1 John 2:16. In this subtle way, the devil has something for everybody. There are those to whom the lusts of the flesh are distasteful, and any temptation along those lines would meet with failure. But such people can be highly susceptible to "the lust of the eyes"—*to have* possessions. Others are easily drawn out on the over-desire of the pride of life—the urge *to be*, with its longing for position.

In Isaiah 14:12-17 we find more about the source of temptation in some remarkable words concerning one who is called "Lucifer, son of the morning." An examination of this passage shows that these words were not applied to a human being, but to one who had access to the heavenly places. We can take these words as an amazing revelation concerning the fall of Satan. We do not know when or where the incident took place. The Bible is once again silent on details that would send our minds wandering on useless speculations. It is sufficient to realize that as far as we need to know, this was the beginning of all temptation.

As we read these verses in Isaiah, we can see clearly indicated those urges which produced the trinity of temptation. Five times the words "I will" appear, and they were all spoken in the heart: "For you have said in your heart . . ." (verse 13). In this connection, it is interesting to note the words of the first verse of Psalms 14 and 53: "The fool has said in his heart, 'There is no God.'" Note also how the Psalmist writes in Psalm 119:11: "Your word I have hidden in my heart, that I might not sin against You." The attitude of the heart leads to the pattern of the life.

The first of Satan's three temptations is "the lust of the flesh." We can see this temptation in Isaiah 14:13— "I will ascend into heaven." This is the desire *to do*. The second temptation is "the lust of the eyes." It is seen in verse 13 also: "I will exalt my throne above the stars of God"—the desire *to have*. The third temptation is "the pride of life." In verse 14 Lucifer said, "I will be like the Most High"—the desire *to be*.

Behind all these urges lay the consuming passion to be independent of God. This one, "Lucifer, son of the morning," was blessed and honored with privileges, position, and potentiality—but somehow it wasn't enough. Verse 15 gives the judgement pronounced upon him: "Yet you shall be brought down to Sheol, to the lowest depths of the Pit." In Matthew 25:41, the Lord Jesus Himself uses these terrible words: ". . . everlasting fire prepared for the devil and his angels." He underlines the twofold fact that the devil has a future place of punishment, and that he was not alone in his desire to be independent of God. The devil was the leader of a movement for independence from God. He was expelled from God's economy, but for some reason known only to the counsels of the Godhead, he was allowed to function as the source of temptation. Thus it is that wherever we see the devil in action, he is always in the process of tempting men, and always with this aim in view—to get men to walk in independence of God.

Romans 14:23 ends with these words: "whatever is not from faith is sin." This is the most inclusive definition of sin in the Bible. Faith is dependence on God. Therefore *whatever is not of faith* is independence of God. Basically then, sin is independence of God— which is exactly what we see in Isaiah 14:12-17. Sin is not an act, or even a series of acts; it is an attitude toward God. This is why the man or woman whose life is morally good and inoffensive is still a sinner. Such a person leaves God out. Even a quality of "goodness" which is independent of God is sin!

This is the reason for the awful condemnation by Christ recorded in Matthew 7:21-23. The Lord Jesus tells how on the Day of judgment there will be those who will seek to establish their "goodness" by saying, "Lord, Lord, have we not prophesied in Your name, cast out demons in Your name, and done many wonders in Your name?" The answer from the lips of Christ will be, "I never knew you; depart from Me, you who practice lawlessness." Christ never knew them; they were operating in independence from Him. So what they had put forward as "good works" He condemned as iniquity. We certainly need to be "broad-minded" on the subject of sin—"broad" in the sense that we understand the implications of independence.

Sin is not an act, or even a series of acts; it is an attitude toward God. Even a quality of "goodness" which is independent of God is sin!

Having thought of the *source* of temptation, we can now go on to consider the *system* of temptation—the application by the devil of his own practices against God's creatures. It is helpful to realize that in the devil's case, independence led to opposition. Having become, in a certain sense, independent from God, he then moved into opposition *against* God. Whenever the devil comes with his temptations, however attractive they may be, he is tempting with one purpose in mind—to strike back at God. He is not in the least concerned with what happens to the victim of his temptation. Once he has achieved his aim of striking at God, he is satisfied. This is a truth we all need to realize—that even Christians can be tools in the hand of Satan, that temptation is basically an attempted act against God, against His divine majesty, and against His compassionate heart of love.

The record of the fall of man is found in Genesis 3. Here is the first recorded act of Satan, when he moved out in opposition to God. Genesis 2 tells of the association between the Lord God and His creatures, how He had provided for them all the things they needed to fulfill their purpose in life, as far as God intended it be lived. God had provided all things, and in return He was seeking their loving obedience. Verses 16 and 17 record how Adam and Eve were to demonstrate their love and obedience. They were forbidden to eat of the tree of the knowledge of good and evil. As they left this tree alone, so they would show their love. But if they ate of the fruit, they would surely die. In this way they were given a choice, and the choice they made would decide the quality of life they would live and experience. It is important here to realize the necessity of choice. There had to be a choice so that love could be demonstrated. It was at this place of choice that the enemy moved in to attack by temptation in chapter three.

There were two parts to the devil's attack—first his tactics, and then his truth. We can see here, as the story unfolds, that this is still the devil's method of approach. Not only does his trinity of temptation remain the same, but also his tactics and his truth.

The first of his tactics was to move in with a doubt. In chapter 3:1, he approached Eve with the question: "Has God indeed said?" Satan did not begin with a downright *denial* of God's Word; he merely cast *doubt* on it. Then when the doubt was not repulsed, he moved in with a lie in verse 4: "You will not surely die." This is exactly how the enemy works today—by casting doubts on the Word of God. There are men in our pulpits today who do his work for him. They say, "Does the Bible really mean this?" Then by expanding the point of doubt, they seek to break the Word. Having gotten people to doubt the Word, they then proceed to deny its teaching. "When the Bible says this, it doesn't really mean this—it means something else!" Any form of Bible preaching which depends on doubts or denials for its success is satanic in its origin. There is nothing new or clever in "finding" errors in God's Word. The first recorded use of the Word of God was to doubt its accuracy and to deny its truth.

Any form of Bible preaching which depends on doubts or denials for its success is satanic in its origin. There is nothing new or clever in finding "errors" in God's Word.

Having completed his tactics, the devil then went on to present his "truth." It is important to realize that the devil has a positive as well as a negative approach. He is a great preacher, and there are many who believe his "truths" and follow his practices. Satan's "truth" is, of course, based on his denial of God's Word. The Lord Jesus said in John 8:44 concerning the devil, that he "does not stand in the truth, because there is no truth in him. When he speaks a lie, he speaks from his own resources, for he is a liar and the father of it." So in Genesis 3:4, the "truth" he presented was a denial: "You will not surely die."

This is the great "truth" the enemy has presented right down through the ages—"Sin, and you can get away with it!" The Bible says, "Be sure your sin will find you out" (Numbers 32:23), but the devil says, "Not so! You will be different; you will get away with it!" No one ever started drinking liquor with the intention of being an alcoholic. Each one says, "Oh, I'm different. I know when to stop. I'll be all right." But they haven't known when to stop. There are many who begin to play with sin under the assumption that they can get away with it, believing the lie of the devil. The tragedy is that each person has to learn this truth for himself—often at great cost. The tragedy of youth is the unwillingness to profit from the lessons learned by others.

Having stated his great "truth" which was a lie, Satan went on to make a wonderful offer: "For God knows that in the day you eat of it your eyes will be opened, and you will be like God." He even brought in the name of God to back up what he was saying—God knows. What a strange invitation—Satan using the name of God to give authority to the lying offer he presents! Every temptation that comes is an invitation to step out into independence from God. This is what Satan was doing here, enticing these two to eat of the forbidden fruit so that they might be as God. No longer would they be dependent on the Lord God for the life that they would live and the decisions they would make. They would be gods themselves, doing what they wanted in the glorious freedom of independence. Fellowship with God was seen as a bondage to be overthrown, and the future as an exciting unknown adventure. *"Your eyes will be opened"* suggests the thrill of the mysterious unseen. They would cease to be childishly simple, and they would move into an area of maturity more fitting to their age and abilities. "*God knows*" suggests that the Lord God knew all this but was keeping something back from them, that they were not getting a fair deal but were being cheated of their rightful possessions.

This is the attitude of many people today who are away from God. Fellowship with God is looked upon as a form of bondage. Becoming a Christian is an act of giving up all the good old freedoms and becoming subject to a code of restrictions. Christians are looked upon as a bunch of immature children who know nothing of the realities of life. They are like newborn kittens—their eyes are not open to the maturity of manhood. The same old satanic lie is still at work today in the hearts of intelligent and cultured men and women.

The devil brought "reality" into his offer by saying that these two would know *good and evil*. The suggestion here is that all they knew so far was "good." Their experience of life had been one-sided and possibly rather dull. "Good" is all right in one sense, but it is so limiting, so frustrating, so naive. If they would just step out into independence and exert their own will for a change, then they would become as gods, and the proof of their godship would be that they would also know evil. Notice that "evil" was presented in the same breath as "good," as an experience of equal value and importance—a mark of maturity, a sign of godlike qualities. The whole idea was that they hadn't begun to live until they were well-aquainted with evil.

This is the great temptation the devil brings to our teenagers and young people today. Young people who are brought up in a Christian home meet this form of attack all along the line. So-called "friends" will say, "Oh, you Christian kids, all you know is good. You are a bunch of goody-goodies. Church two or three times on Sunday, and even during the week! You've never lived, you haven't seen real life yet. You come with us, and we'll show you things that will open your eyes. Come and get a real kick out of life. Enjoy yourself while you're young!" The pressures exerted are exactly the same as those initiated in Genesis 3. Young people are called upon to step out in independence, to throw off parental restrictions and all moral restraints, to become "mature." Good and evil are still put together; evil isn't wrong, it is just a form of self-expression, a vindication of individuality, a proof that I am growing up. The devil's basic tactics and truth are as successful today as they ever were.

9

The Secret Of Overcoming Temptation

In the previous chapter, when we discussed the secret of recognizing temptation, we considered the devil's trinity of temptation as set forth in 1 John 2:16: "the lust of the flesh, the lust of the eyes, and the pride of life." This is the devil's blueprint on which he bases all his attacks on the human heart. If we continue with our story as told in Genesis 3:6, we can see this clearly demonstrated.

"So when the woman saw that the tree was good for food, that it was pleasant to the eyes, and a tree desirable to make one wise, she took of its fruit and ate. She also gave to her husband with her, and he ate."

This first thing the woman saw was a *tree good for food*. The Lord God had provided amply for all their needs—there was more than enough food for them. There was no need for any outside supplementation. But James 1:14 tells us that "each one is tempted when he is drawn away by his own desires and enticed." The Bible teaches here that temptation arises not from without, but from within, from the heart of man. So it was that Eve was tempted first by the lust of the flesh, the over-desire of the flesh.

The second thing the woman saw was a tree *pleasant to the eyes*. Here we see the second thrust of Satan's attack—the lust or over-desire of the eyes. With the third prong of the attack, she saw that it was "a tree desirable to make one wise." Here we see *the pride of life*. Eve was drawn to a quality of wisdom which comes from disobeying God, whereas Proverbs 9:10 teaches that "the fear of the Lord is the beginning of wisdom, and the knowledge of the Holy One is understanding." Here again we see the lie of the devil. He suggested that the knowing of evil would make them as gods, whereas the Bible teaches that the knowing of the Holy One is the beginning of real wisdom and understanding.

The original sin was the decision to step out into independence. This is the basic sin in every human heart today.

It is important to see that the taking of the fruit was not the actual sin. The decision had already been made in the heart; the taking of the fruit was but an outward expression of an inward attitude. The original sin was the decision to step out into independence. This is the basic sin in every human heart today.

It is interesting to note that the Bible begins and ends with this warning of the devil's trinity of temptation. It is found in Genesis 3 at the beginning of the Bible. It is also recorded in 1 John 2:16, the last letter written to all believers.

Just as the Old Testament begins with the story of Adam's temptation by Satan, so the New Testament begins with Christ's temptation by Satan. Three of the gospels record it (Matthew 4, Mark 1, Luke 4). Adam and Eve were tempted in the midst of plenty and in a place of perfection; the Lord Jesus was tempted in the wilderness. Our first parents had all they needed, with much to spare, but the Lord had fasted for forty days and forty nights. Matthew 4:2 gives us this vivid understatement: "afterward He was hungry."

In considering the story of the temptation as recorded in Matthew, Mark, and Luke, we should be careful to remember from where they got their story. Only Christ and Satan were present throughout the hours of temptation. Therefore, the written account as we have it must have come directly from the lips of Christ Himself. It was the Lord Jesus who told us that after the temptation He was hungry. The physical sufferings were real and intense, and were written deep in His memory. These temptations were not theological discussions taking place in the study or the school room; they were physical, mental, and spiritual battles fought out in the heat and cold of the wilderness.

The picture presented in Genesis is one of miserable failure. The human heart, faced with the choice, chose to step into open independence. The picture presented in the temptation of Christ is one of glorious victory, a victory based on dependence. The secret of overcoming temptation is shown in the barren wilderness; the sorrow of failure is seen in the beautiful garden.

The most blessed thing about the victory of Christ is that it was based, not upon superhuman power or divine miracles, but upon faith and dependence upon God. If the Lord Jesus had won His victory through angelic intervention or by exerting His divine authority, then there would have been no example for us to follow. We might have looked and longed for such success, but with no possible hope of experiencing such a victory. The Lord Jesus used nothing that is not available to us. His weapon was the Word of God, and His power was His utter dependence upon His Father.

The most blessed thing about the victory of Christ is that it was based, not upon superhuman power or divine miracles, but upon faith and dependence upon God.

At this point it is good to learn the great truth that it is not a sin to be tempted. The sin lies not in the temptation, but in my response to that temptation. The proof of this truth is the fact that the Lord Jesus was tempted in all things as we are, but He was without sin. The devil often comes to young people and strikes at them because they have experienced temptation. He suggests that because they have found themselves in these situations, or because these thoughts and ideas have come to their minds, then they are already guilty by association. This is not true. Sin only emerges as I allow the temptation to find an answering echo in my own heart. The purest heart that ever lived faced temptation, yet it emerged clean and pure.

There is also a line of thought which imagines that the Lord Jesus was tempted only these three times. These are three classical *examples* of temptation. But

Luke 4:13 in the Amplified Bible reads, "And when the devil had ended every [the complete cycle of] temptation, he [temporarily] left Him [that is, stood off from Him] until another more opportune *and* favorable time." The Lord was constantly meeting the power of the tempter, but He possessed the wonderful secret of overcoming temptation.

When Satan came to tempt Christ, he had had many years of successful practice. No one had ever been able to resist completely all his schemes and devices. With all that power, he moved in to attack the Lord Jesus in His moment of greatest physical weakness. The devil never had a more favorable situation in which to work.

His ultimate aim was to tempt Christ to act in His own strength, to entice Him to step out in independence. Satan began his attack on Christ in the same way as he began his attack on Eve—by casting doubt on the Word of God. To Eve he said "Has God indeed said?" (Genesis 3:1). When she listened to the doubt, he followed up with the lie. To the Lord Jesus, his first words were, "If You are the Son of God" (Matthew 4:3). The devil was doing then what he is busy doing today—sowing doubts about the deity of Christ.

The temptation was so simple, but so sly: "If You are the Son of God, command that these stones become bread." The eating of bread by a starving man isn't a sin. It is just the satisfying of a natural hunger. The turning of stones into bread was not outside the power of Him who turned corrupt flesh into living humanity. But for Christ to initiate a special process in personal independence would be against all that Jesus stood for, and contradict all He would ever say or teach.

"Then Jesus answered and said to them, 'Most assuredly, I say to you, the Son can do nothing of Himself, but what He sees the Father do; for whatever He does, the Son also does in like manner. . . . I can of myself do nothing. . . . because I do not seek My own will but the will of the Father who sent Me (John 5:19, 30)."

"Jesus answered them and said, 'My doctrine is not mine, but His who sent Me" (John 7:16).

"Philip . . . do you not believe that I am in the Father, and the Father in Me? The words that I speak to you I do not speak on My own authority; but the Father who dwells in Me does the works (John 14:9, 10)."

The first man, Adam, fell because he chose to walk in independence. The last Adam gloriously fulfilled all the will and purposes of God because He chose to submit and subject Himself to His Father every step of the way. He summed it up in John 8:29: "I always do those things that please Him."

The subtlety and thrust of this first temptation then was to get the Lord to meet the natural needs of His body through His own divine ability—to act without the Father.

One of the greatest lessons we can learn about the secret of overcoming temptation is to see how it was that the Lord Jesus met and handled the situation. It is here that we find our greatest comfort. If the Lord had overcome by superhuman power or by angelic intervention, then there would be no message of comfort for us. We would simply realize that He was the Son of God—God manifest in the flesh—and that His deity had won Him the victory. But the wonder is that Christ never availed Himself of His deity in meeting these problems. The weapons the Lord used in the battle are free for us to use. He showed us the secret by the example of His victory.

The Lord Jesus used nothing more than the written Word of God. He took its teaching and its truth as His answer, and rested in simple faith on what God had said. This is both the privilege and possibility of even the youngest believer today. One needs no argument, no depth of wisdom, no skill in doctrine—just the simple handling of the Word of God. The Lord

---

The first man, Adam, fell because he chose to walk in independence. The last Adam gloriously fulfilled all the will and purposes of God because He chose to submit and subject Himself to His Father every step of the way.

---

answered each of the three temptations by quoting Scripture. And it is interesting to find that He quoted each time from the same book, Deuteronomy—a book often overlooked or ignored by believers today. The Lord clearly demonstrated the truth of Psalm 119:11: "Your word I have hidden in my heart, that I might not sin against You." It was the hidden word that won the victory over Satan.

Satan came to Eve with the first of his trinity of temptations—the lust of the flesh. In the same way, he came to Christ. The greatest need in the human body of Christ at that specific moment was food to meet the bitter pangs of hunger. Eve met her temptation in the place of plenty and with a body replete and satisfied—

she had no immediate need crying out to be met. The desires of the flesh must have been strong in the weakened body of Christ, but His answer came, "Man shall not live by bread alone; but man lives by every word that proceeds from the mouth of the Lord" (quoted from Deuteronomy 8:3). There was something more important than satisfying the hunger of the body—willingness to walk in dependence and obedience to the revealed Word of God.

In his second temptation, the devil approached through the lust of the eye. He took Jesus to the pinnacle of the temple from where it was possible to see the thousands of faithful Jews thronging the courts below. They were coming to worship, and—here was the point of the temptation—if Christ were to cast Himself down from the pinnacle, everyone below in the temple courts and busy streets would see Him. They would see the angels bearing Him up as He slowly descended into the temple area. The response would be immediate and complete. They would recognize His deity and would fall down and worship Him. Peace and blessing would abound, and they would all live happily ever after.

But this was not the will of God for Christ. Isaiah 53 had spoken for hundreds of years of a Savior who was going to be despised and rejected, who was going to be wounded and put to death. If Christ had sought success Satan's way, it would have been in complete independence from God's will and Word. If the Jews had worshiped Him then, they would never have taken Him to Pilate for execution. If the Lord Jesus had not died on the cross, then He could never have been our blessed Savior. Satan offered the Lord success without suffering, something he constantly offers believers today—quick results with nothing to worry about!

It is important also to see the very words used by Satan to bring this second attack. The answer of Christ to the first temptation had been, "It is written, 'Man shall not live by bread alone. . . .'" Immediately Satan follows up by saying, "it is written, 'He shall give His angels charge over you. . . .'" As he did to Eve, Satan quoted Scripture to prove his point. See how

---

Satan offered the Lord success without suffering, something he constantly offers believers today—quick results with nothing to worry about!

---

subtle his suggestion was. The Lord had just said that a man ought to live by trusting God's Word, so the devil replied—"Exactly, and here is your chance to prove it! Commit yourself to God's promises, and He will sustain you." This was a truly devilish suggestion. However, a careful examination of the words quoted by Satan shows a revealing thing. In quoting from Psalm 91:11-12 (even the devil can quote Scripture!), he used only as much of the verses as he wanted to prove his point. He misquoted Scripture on purpose, by leaving out the words, "to keep You in all Your ways." The faith that Christ had in God's Word was keeping Him even in that situation on the top of the Temple. The devil doesn't mind people having an academic faith in God's Word, and in the future, as long as he has their obedience in the present.

The answer of Christ to this suggestion was "You shall not tempt the Lord your God" (verse 7). These words were quoted from Deuteronomy 6:16, and they refer to the incident at Massah recorded in Exodus 17:1-7. The whole point of the story at Massah revolved around the question the children of Israel asked there: "Is the Lord among us or not?" (verse 7). They were demanding proof of the presence of God, but Christ was not going to tempt God in that way. He said later to the Jews (John 8:29), "the Father has not left Me alone." Jesus was content, wherever He was, to be dependent on this truth.

The devil doesn't mind people having an academic faith in God's Word, and in the future, as long as he has their obedience in the present.

The third temptation was concerned with the pride of life, the desire for glory and power. "Again, the devil took Him up on an exceedingly high mountain, and showed Him all the kingdoms of the world and their glory" (verse 8). Having shown the Lord Jesus all the power and majesty, the devil said to Him, "All these things I will give You, if You will fall down and worship me." It is good to remember that the devil only deals in *things*. "All these things," he offered Jesus—the lure of the material. But the Lord Jesus knew and taught that "one's life does not consist in the abundance of the things which he possesses" (Luke 12:15).

The devil also offered these things to Jesus at a very low price: "If You will worship me," he said. One simple act of recognition, with no one else around to see, would be sufficient to receive all the power and the glory of the world. Notice, incidentally, that the Lord did not deny the devil's claim to these worldly possessions. He accepted his claim, even as He called Satan on two occasions "the ruler of this world" (John 14:30; 16:11). The devil was prepared to trade all the world's wealth for a simple moment of acknowledgment—or so he seemed to suggest.

But the craftiness behind his words was revealed by the answer of Christ in verse 10: "You shall worship the Lord your God, and Him only you shall serve." Here the Lord Jesus shows us a tremendous truth: worship and service go together. You serve that which you worship. True worship of God involves service to God. Similarly, any worship or acknowledgment of Satan involves service to Satan. Satan had only asked for worship, but Christ knew that anyone who worships Satan will soon be in bondage to him.

Thus it was that, with nothing more than the Word of God and a perfect faith and trust in that Word, the Lord Jesus was able to win a victory over Satan, even in this moment of physical exhaustion. The teaching here is so wonderfully simple. Temptation is not overcome on the basis of my strong will, or on my long experience, or on my excellent education. It is only overcome when I recognize that of myself I can do nothing. When I trust in the presence of Christ and rest in His Word, then I can share a similar victory.

This truth is made especially clear in the words of Christ to His disciples in Matthew 16:24: "If anyone desires to come after Me, let him deny himself, and take up his cross, and follow me." Following Christ, which includes overcoming temptation, involved three things. Just as the devil had his trinity of temptation, so Christ put forward His trinity of triumph. The devil used *the lust of the flesh, the lust of the eyes, and the pride of life.* The Lord Jesus asks His followers to *"deny himself, and take up his cross, and follow me."* It is interesting to see how the words of Christ provide the correct answer for each thrust of Satan.

The answer to the lust of the flesh is *let him deny himself.* When the over-desires of the body surge into power, Christ instructed His disciples to deny that self, to say "I am not my own. I have been bought with a price. The choice is not mine to make. Not my will, but Yours be done." Having recognized these thoughts, then I act on the basis of them, with the Word of God in my heart and in my life.

The answer to the lust of the eyes is to *take up the cross.* This is what it meant for Christ in His temptation. He chose not to have any success that came without suffering. He chose the cross. And this is His word for us—*take up your cross.* In some churches the cross is often a beautiful thing of brass or gold. Sometimes it is even studded with precious stones—a thing to be admired and sometimes worshiped. The cross is sometimes also a small symbol to wear on a necklace or brooch.

But this is not the cross Christ wants us to take up. The cross was a cruel, ugly thing, a stark fact to be avoided and an unpleasant situation to be shunned. The cross wasn't made to be worshiped or worn. It was made for one purpose only—to die on! The answer to the lust of the eyes is to take up the cross, with all its finality. Victory for Christ came only through the cross. In like manner we, too, will only experience victory over temptation when we are crucified with Christ, when we reckon ourselves dead to sin but alive to God through our Lord Jesus Christ.

The answer to the pride of life is simply this—*follow Me.* Following Christ in example, in death, in teaching, and in His risen power is the only answer to the pull of the world's glory and honor. Not that a Christian should never be in a position of authority or power—God has many of His children in high places. If this is God's will for a person then that is the place of God, and he will surely experience the power of God. Such a place will have come through dependence only on God. The pride of life is the full pressure *from within*, not from above. Christ's answer is "Follow Me." He told His disciples, "I am the light of the world. He who follows Me shall not walk in darkness, but have the light of life" (John 8:12). If I follow the light, my pathway is clear and the shadows are behind me. If I turn my back on the light and walk the other way, I walk in a pathway that is not illuminated. I walk in the shadow, and it is a shadow cast by me as I put the light behind me.

Temptation is always a pull and a pressure to be independent of God. The only answer to it is the one voiced by Ruth: "For wherever you go, I will go; and wherever you lodge, I will lodge; your people shall be my people, and your God, my God. Where you die, I will die, and there will I be buried. The Lord do so to me, and more also, if anything but death parts you and me." (Ruth 1:16-17).

10

The Secret Of Meeting Sorrow

One of the greatest tests of any Christian's faith is the problem of sorrow and suffering, tragedy and disaster. These things are real. They hurt, and they cause doubts and questions to arise in the hearts of many of God's people. So often we ask the question "Why?"—not only about our own lives, but also about the lives of others. We see a young husband or wife taken, and the spouse left with a family of little ones. We see children grow up to break the hearts of their wonderful Christian parents. We see a really effective witness for God crushed, with no chance of recovery. These and a thousand other realities come as savage blows to our faith, and our hearts are troubled. Has God forgotten? Does God really care?

I remember once being helped by a very effective visual aid. First we were shown a painting of a lovely sunlit country scene. There was color and shape and composition—all beautifully balanced—but somehow the result didn't seem real. There was a sense that something was missing in the picture. Then we were shown the exact same picture as it should really have been. The missing ingredients were there, and the painting was complete. As we compared the two pictures, we saw what had been missing—the shadows.

The first picture was a blaze of joyous light, but there wasn't a shadow anywhere. As a result the scene was unreal; it lacked depth. The second painting had deep, long shadows, penetrating far into the whole scene— and it was real. It takes shadows to give balance, reality, depth, and contrast to painting.

What is true in painting is equally true in daily living. The sorrows and tragedies of life are the shadows which give it depth, reality, and contrast. While this describes the situation and puts it in correct balance, it in no way gives us the answer. What is the secret of meeting sorrow and distress? Does God have an answer to the broken heart?

We can be helped if we look into the Word of God and see the whole question dealt with in three ways. Three different words are used in Scripture to describe three different qualities of suffering. Each word opens up a line of approach which can help us understand something of the secret of meeting suffering.

The first word is *tribulation*. It occurs twenty-one times in the New Testament and is loaded with meaning. It comes from the Latin word *tribulum,* meaning a Roman threshing instrument used to beat the piled-up ears of wheat. The repeated blows of the tribulum separated the wheat from the chaff, leaving behind the valuable grain. The word *tribulation* gives us a picture, then, of *pressure from without* beating down upon us— but it is pressure with a purpose. The tribulum did not senselessly beat the air, but the wheat, which eventually provided bread for the hungry and further seed for the sower.

This is beautifully set forth in 2 Corinthians 1:3-4: "Blessed be the God and Father of our Lord Jesus Christ, the Father of mercies and the God of all comfort, who comforts us in all our tribulation, that we may be able to comfort those who are in any trouble, with the comfort with which we ourselves are comforted of God."

The first purpose of tribulation, as taught in these verses, is that we might experience *the comfort of God.* The five-fold use of the word *comfort* here is very significant. The comfort of God is not the same as the love of God. All believers experience the love of God, but not all Christians experience the comfort of God. The comfort of God is something very precious and very real—but it is only experienced in tribulation, when pressures beat down from without.

The word *comfort* today has changed its meaning. As we use it, we convey the thought of sympathy, that "we are sorry this has happened, and we hope it will

---

The comfort of God is something very precious and very real—but it is only experienced in tribulation, when pressures beat down from without.

---

soon be better." But *comfort* originally meant much more. It comes from the Latin *fortis* which means strength and power. Our word *fort* comes from it, too. A fort is a place of strength and power. In the early days of the settlers, people could go to the fort for protection, and the cavalry would ride out from the fort to attack. In the Bible, the word *comfort* denotes the bringing of power and strength. The Lord Jesus Himself chose to call the Holy Spirit "the Comforter" (John 14:16, 26; 15:26; 16:7).

This, then, is the implication in 2 Corinthians 1:4—"who comforts us in all our tribulation." The God of comfort draws near to us in a new and special way, and we experience a new quality of strength and power as we are being beaten down by suffering caused by pressures from without. "The eternal God is your refuge, and underneath are the everlasting arms" (Deuteronomy 33:27). Notice where the everlasting arms are—underneath us. This verse fits in beautifully with the thoughts we have been considering. The pressures from above may force me down, but *underneath are the everlasting arms.* The lower I go, the nearer I go to the arms of the God of all comfort. If I reach rock bottom, then I am in the arms of my wonderful Heavenly Father.

But these verses in 2 Corinthians teach us more than that we should experience the comfort of God. The purpose of our experience is "that we may be able to comfort those who are in any trouble, with the comfort with which we ourselves are comforted of God" (verse 4). The thought here is that we should be able to share the comfort of God with others. Our own tribulation qualifies us to speak to others of the love and grace and comfort of God.

Some time ago, a young married woman told me of an incident in her experience. In the town where she lived there had been a recent tragedy. A two-year-old boy had wandered into the street not far from where she lived, and had been killed in the rush of passing traffic. His mother was heartbroken. He was her only child. She wasn't a church-going person, and she and her husband were truly broken by the tragedy. The neighbors came to the sorrowing mother, seeking to comfort her with sympathy and simple acts of kindness, but her grief was so severe that nothing could help her. When the friends spoke to her she replied, "You don't understand, you don't know how I feel!"

This went on for several weeks. The young mother seemed unable to deal with her tragedy. "Then," my friend said, "I really felt the Lord telling me to go and speak to this brokenhearted girl. I didn't know her, except by sight, and at first I was reluctant to impose myself on her sorrow." However, as she prayed about it she felt that this was indeed the will of God for her. So one morning she went. Approaching the door, she felt very nervous and at a complete loss to know how to handle the situation. With a word of prayer in her heart, she knocked gently on the door and waited. Presently the door was opened, and there stood the young mother, pale and red-eyed. My friend told me, "As I stood there I could find no words to say, but in tender love I opened my arms to her. She paused a moment, looked at me, recognized me, and then came into my arms. As she clung close to me she sobbed 'Oh, you understand, you understand.'"

I looked at my friend, wondering what she meant. "You see," she said, "I lost my little boy the same way last year!" My friend went on to say that she had been able to have many conversations with the young mother. She had told her of her faith in God and of how God had comforted her when she lost her son last year. She had been able to take the girl and her husband to church, and they were attending regularly. Finally she said, "I don't think it will be long now before they both trust Christ." Then, after a pause, she added, "Wouldn't it be strange if they found Christ because my little son was killed?"

I remember how deeply moved I was by her simple story. Here was the Scripture being fulfilled! She had experienced the comfort of God, and in a wonderful way had shared that comfort—to the glory of God.

The second word we can consider is one that refers to *pain within*. In 2 Corinthians 12:7-10, Paul tells his readers about a *thorn in the flesh* which had been given to him. This section contains rich teaching on the secret of meeting suffering. Many ideas have been put forward as to the mystery of this thorn in the flesh.

What matters most in our lives in the long run is not the circumstances in which we find ourselves, but our reaction to those circumstances.

Some have thought it was Paul's trouble with his eyes. Others have suggested leprosy, and others a lump on his back. But the Bible has seen fit to leave the nature of the "thorn" a mystery. This is good, because it points our interest away from the actual complaint and centers our thoughts on Paul's reaction to the whole situation. The emphasis is valuable to us, because what matters most in our lives in the long run is not the circumstances in which we find ourselves, but our reaction to those circumstances.

This same thorn can help us to appreciate more thoroughly God's sovereignty in healing and deliverance. God *can* heal and *does* heal, and He delivers in many wonderful ways. But several incidents in the Bible indicate that God does so in His sovereign grace alone, and this is one of them. If any man had faith, it was Paul. So if healing or deliverance was dependent upon the exercise of faith, then Paul would have been sure of God's assistance. If any man deserved to be healed, it was Paul. But God chose not to answer his prayers the way Paul requested. In like manner, when Paul left Trophimus sick at Miletum (2 Timothy 4:20), God did not heal him. In 1 Timothy 5:23, Paul gave Timothy advice on treating his sickness rather than praying for healing.

There are three things we can learn from the thorn in the flesh—its peculiarity, its purpose, and its plan.

First let us see the peculiarity of this thorn. There are two separate words used in the Bible which are translated as "thorn." One is *akantha*, from which we get the name acanthus—a very thorny shrub. This word is the one generally used in the Bible, denoting a thorn or a briar. It indicates the kind of sharp thorn that grows on a rose.

There is another word translated "thorn," the word *skolops*. The word is only used once in the whole Bible, in this very passage. It denotes a sharp stake, such as is used to make a fence. Paul implies, therefore, that his thorn in the flesh was something severe—not a mere thorn or prickle in the finger, but a sharp pointed stake going right through his body. This, Paul says, was "the messenger of Satan." It was because of the pain within, the agony, the frustration, and the restriction it brought that Paul cried to God three times to have the thing removed.

When we stop to consider the purpose of this thorn in the flesh, we find certain remarkable factors. First, the thorn did not hinder the purpose of God. Although there was a shortage of great preachers in that day, God's purposes were not frustrated because one of the greatest preachers was suffering so acutely. In fact, Paul's thorn became part of God's purpose. What an amazing thing that God's program for the evangelization of the world at that time was largely dependent on a man who was in such desperate need of deliverance. Here is a tremendous lesson for us today. We tend to operate on the assumption that God can only bless when everything is just right, that if we are not one hundred percent up to par in every way, then God's work is going to suffer. It wasn't so with Paul.

As we go on to consider the plan in which the thorn was involved, we see some strange facts. Paul's obvious plan was, "I could serve you so much better if I were free from this thorn. I would have more strength and more endurance, so that I could be much more effective." But God's amazing answer to him was—*"My strength is made perfect in your weakness."* Paul had imagined that God's strength would be made perfect in Paul's strength. But not so. God's strength was to be perfected in Paul's *weakness*. In other words, God was saying, "Paul, you are more use to me with the thorn than without it!"

This is why Paul responds so wonderfully: "Therefore most gladly I will rather boast in my infirmities, that the power of Christ may rest upon me. Therefore I take pleasure in infirmities, in reproaches, in needs, in persecutions, in distresses, for Christ's sake. For when I am weak, then am I strong (2 Cor. 12:9-10)."

What brave, wonderful words. What an answer to the problem of pain within. Not "Why the pain?" but "What is the plan in the heart of God behind the pain?" Here is the faith that recognized that God sometimes uses thorns to fulfil His purposes, the faith that looks at the cross of Christ and sees that even the Lord Jesus Christ wore a crown—of thorns. Here indeed is one of the greatest challenges to our faith— that God sometimes uses our suffering to achieve His purpose. If, by His grace, I can see my pain as part of God's plan—even if I cannot understand it—then somehow the shadows give depth and reality to life, and I take my place in the panorama of God.

The question is not "Why the pain?" but "What is the plan in the heart of God behind the pain?"

During a visit to wonderful Marine Land in San Diego, California, I learned a valuable lesson on the provision of God. A section of Marine Land is devoted to the culture of pearls. I was able to see from the exhibits on view exactly how a natural pearl was formed. First there is the oyster. Then into the oyster's shell is introduced a substance which becomes a source of great irritation and suffering—a small stone or some other foreign body. Once this irritation is in the oyster, it is there for good. It is a real thorn in the flesh for the oyster, but the creature has to live with it. Yet God has provided the oyster with a wonderful way of handling the source of suffering. The creature is able to manu- facture a wondrously smooth material with which it covers the irritation. This protective covering is what makes the actual pearl. As the years go by, the oyster continues to cover the "problem" with more precious pearl material so that, in God's good time, this "thing" which came in originally as an irritant or a thorn, becomes transformed.

So I learned, in a wonderful way, that a precious pearl is really a problem covered with the provision of God. This is what Paul learned, what many of God's people have learned down the ages. Life without the provision of Christ is often just a string of sorrows and tragedies and sufferings. But, praise God, when these problems are covered with what He has provided, the string of problems becomes instead a string of pearls.

It is interesting to read in Revelation 21 the description of the New Jerusalem. Having completed a wonderful picture of the glorious new city, John describes the entrances to the city in verse 21: "And the twelve gates were twelve pearls: each individual gate was of one pearl." The only way into the city is through a pearl, the symbol of pain covered by the provision of God. I know many Christians in this world whose lives are spent in much physical pain. But, somehow, God has touched them and the pain has become a pearl—and the pearl has become a gate through which others have entered into eternal life.

We saw in the section on tribulation—pressure without—that the purpose of this suffering was two-fold: to experience the comfort of God, and then to share the comfort of God. The purpose of the suffering of the thorn—pain within—is also two-fold: to experience the power of God, and then to demonstrate the power of God.

The third word we are going to consider is the word *chastening*. In Hebrews 12:1-13, the author challenges his readers to "lay aside every weight, and the sin which so easily ensnares us, and let us run with endurance the race that is set before us. . . . You have not yet resisted to bloodshed, striving against sin" (verses 1, 4). The whole section is an urgent call for a purer quality of living, and for a more tenacious quality of enduring. Verses 5-11 develop the idea of chastening. Seven times in these seven verses this word is thrust at us, demanding our immediate attention. Chastening is connected to the problems *around* us. We are called upon not to despise the chastening of the Lord (verse 5). We are told that "whom the Lord loves He chastens" (verse 6), and that if we are without chastisement then we are not true sons (verse 8).

The great mistake we can make here is to suppose that chastening is the same as punishment, and thereby to imagine that in some strange way God is going to punish us whatever happens. This kind of thinking then interprets the problems around as the way God is punishing. Some dear souls get so worked up, seeing the awful hand of God punishing them when things go wrong. This type of reasoning loses all the wonder and joy and true purpose of being a child of God.

Chastening involves training, teaching, and instruction rather than punishment. It is linked with the thought of a purer quality of living and a more effective quality of enduring. When a soldier is new to his job, he has to undergo much teaching, training, and instruction. He may have to spend hours of intensive training on an assault course where he climbs steep obstacles and is stretched physically in order to improve his powers of endurance. But none of this is punishment. It is all part of the job of being a soldier. The more elite his regiment, the harder will be his training. If he is a marine, some of his instruction will involve pain and hardship and considerable danger—

but no one complains. These men are dedicated to a task. They *expect* to be stretched and wearied and exhausted, all for a purpose. This is real chastening, to turn boys into men, and men into marines!

Hebrews 12 calls us to lay aside every weight and to run the race set before us. In other words, we need to spend more time on our training as soldiers of the cross. We need firmer muscles, more responsive obedience, and a brave heart that does not flinch when under the enemy's fire. All this comes through chastening.

Verses 10 and 11 tell us why we undergo this chastening. First—*that we may be partakers of His holiness*. It is sad to realize that one of the greatest weaknesses in the Church today is a lack of the sense of God's holiness. The Old Testament's over-ruling theme is the holiness of God. The Temple worship was geared to this end. The Ten Commandments were

---

It is sad to realize that one of the greatest weaknesses in the Church today is a lack of the sense of God's holiness.

---

based on this one great factor. But today we have lost much of this supreme wonder of our faith—that *our God is a Holy God*. We need to be constantly "cut down to size," to realize our own unimportance, to learn to respond to the greatness of God.

Although chastening is not pleasant, "afterward it yields the peaceable fruit of righteousness to those who have been trained by it" (verse 11). The fruit of chastisement is a righteous life which enjoys the peace of God. I have peace in my soul because my life is right with God, because I have put first things first, because I have humbled my heart before a Holy God. Notice that these things happen to those who "have been trained by it." In other words, we have to work at it, and let chastening work in us. We have to face up to our problems and situations, recognizing that this is how God is training us for the tasks ahead. All this is part of chastening, the simple realization that the events of my life, the problems that meet me daily, are part of God's great battle training program for my life.

This is what Isaac Watts meant when he wrote:

> "Am I a soldier of the cross,
> A follower of the Lamb?
> And shall I fear to own His cause,
> Or blush to speak His name?
>
> Must I be carried to the skies
> On flowery beds of ease,
> While others fought to win the prize,
> And sailed thro' bloody seas?
>
> Are there no foes for me to face?
> Must I not stem the flood?
> Is this vile world a friend to grace,
> To help me on to God?
>
> Sure I must fight, if I would reign;
> Increase my courage, Lord;
> I'll bear the toil, endure the pain,
> Supported by Thy Word."

Part of the secret of meeting sorrow, then, is to recognize it as a means to an end. Each time I stand in the strength of Christ, I grow in His strength. So then, "strengthen the hands which hang down, and the feeble knees" (verse 12).

Paul's great words in Ephesians 6:13 are much to the point: "Therefore take up the whole armor of God, that you may be able to withstand in the evil day, and having done all, to stand."

11

The Secret Of Growing Spiritual Muscles

There is a great desire in the hearts of many people these days to be physically fit—really and effectively physically fit. To achieve this aim, certain foods are avoided and other special foods are encouraged. Advertising cashes in on this desire by selling bread which is "fortified and enriched with added vitamins," and milk that has been "homogenized, pasteurized, enriched with added minerals and vitamins." Beaches and swimming pools are frequented by young men whose muscular bodies are both a challenge and an encouragement to other males to get to work on their muscles so that their bodies will also ripple with hidden power. It is a well-known fact that many men whose bodies were once skinny and weak have become glowing pictures of strength and vitality—all through a serious application of the secret of growing physical muscles. All this can be good in many ways, and for the well-being of the nation as a whole.

In like manner, it is possible to get to work on the *spiritual* muscles of our lives to produce similar results in a spiritual sense. How wonderful it is to see a Christian whose life is simply glowing with spiritual health, tackle heavy loads and burdens, and somehow make short and easy work of handling them. The development of physical muscles is mainly confined to young men—old men and ladies are supposed to stand back and admire. But in the world of spiritual muscles, anyone can be involved. Some of the strongest Christians are those who are no longer young. The mission field is proof enough of the way in which women can go on to become the strongest of the strong.

The Bible has much to say about the secret of growing spiritual muscles. A good place to start is 1 John 2:12-14, where John refers to three groups— little children, young men, and fathers. These are not groups according to physical age, but divisions which reveal progression in spiritual maturity.

It is good to relate the first group, little children, to the teaching of Christ in John 3: 3,7. Here the Lord was dealing with Nicodemus, a man of great moral stature and excellent religious standing. To this man, who was so upright in the eyes of the world, the Lord brought His pointed teaching on the necessity of being born again. Although Nicodemus was morally good and had much to offer, the Lord told him "That which is born of the flesh is flesh, and that which is born of the Spirit is spirit" (verse 6). Nicodemus in himself was just "the flesh," and all his excellence was just the perfection of the flesh. Spiritually he was dead, because there was an absence of spiritual life in his being. When a man is born again, he receives a new quality of life—eternal life—through the indwelling of the Spirit of Christ. Remember that Jesus *is* the Life, as He said in John 14:6: "I am the way, the truth, and the life. No one comes to the Father except through Me."

We can compare the rebirth of the human soul to the physical birth of a baby. Each person begins his physical life as a baby, a child. To receive spiritual life, one must become as a little child: "Unless you are converted and become as little children, you will by no means enter the kingdom of heaven," said Jesus (Matthew 18:3). We can carry the analogy still further. A healthy newborn babe begins to grow physically and continues growing through all the acquired skills of sitting, crawling, and walking; recognizing, responding, and speaking. As the years go by, he attends school and develops more skills. Normal growth takes the little child through the succeeding stages of older child, teenager, and adult. All this is normal and expected. The little child will go on to become a young man or woman, and then a father or mother— in God's good time.

But sometimes the abnormal occurs, and a child does not develop those necessary skills which lead to adult life. One of the most pathetic sights in the world is to see an adult with the brain of a little child—large of limb and strong in body, but a brain that can cope only with the world of a four-year-old. This is not normal, and when it happens special measures are necessary because life is not designed to operate under such unbalanced conditions. These special measures involve more attention, more nursing, more provision, but with no possible hope of the "child's" accepting responsibility.

Hebrews 5:12-13 refers to certain Christians who were still babes in their spiritual growth, who needed to be fed on milk. 1 Corinthians 3:1-3 also refers to the same kind of Christians, still being fed on milk. Their behavior was characterized by all the limitations of babyhood. They were unreliable in their responses, unreasonable in their demands, and unable to accept responsibility or to make decisions. They had never grown up; they were still babies.

The tragedy is that this condition exists today. In many of our churches there are men and women who trusted Christ years ago but who are still babes in Christ. They are spiritual abnormalities. Because of their age, status and social position, people expect to see in them honest, mature Christian living—but they do not. Many pastors have to spend valuable time caring for Christians who don't or won't grow up, who need careful nursing and handling, like small children. They are easily upset and always demand their own way. They sulk if their will is crossed, and they can never be trusted to take responsibility or produce results beneficial to the Church as a whole. They have been born again, but have been content to stay little children.

Many pastors have to spend valuable time caring for Christians who don't or won't grow up, who need careful nursing and handling, like small children.

In this passage in 1 John 2, John says he is writing to the little children because they know two things: "because your sins are forgiven you for His name's sake" (verse 12), "because you have known the Father" (verse 13). They know their sins are forgiven and they know their Heavenly Father. This is wonderful knowledge to possess. All the basis of assurance and safety is there. But it is not enough knowledge with which to go out and do exploits for God. There is no knowledge of the Son, and no capacity for service.

In like manner it is possible for a seeker to come to Christ, to experience forgiveness of sins, to know that God now loves them, and then to stop there. Without prayer and Bible study, their muscles remain flabby and their spiritual limbs continue as the limbs of little children—incapable of sustained effort or of successful service. Such Christians are a headache to their friends and a heartache to their pastor. When such people hold office in their church there are troublesome times ahead for the other officers, because God never intended that babies should stay babies, or that they should hold office in the Church.

God never intended that babies should stay babies, or that they should hold office in the Church.

The information in 1 John concerning the young men is much more exciting. "I have written to you, young men, because you are strong, and the word of God abides in you, and you have overcome the wicked one (verse 14)." The Bible teaches that three things characterize young men: they are strong, the Word of God abides in them, and they have overcome the devil. You cannot be a young man without having first been a little child, so to the threefold abilities of the young man must be added the two-fold knowledge of the little child. Such a development in Christian maturity is one of the crying needs in the Church today—that Christians should go on to develop spiritual muscles, to relate the Word of God to their daily living, and to experience victory day by day.

There is an excellent illustration of a man developing spiritual muscles and winning victories for God in the story of Joshua as told in Joshua 1:1-9. The chapter opens with the stark statement of the death of Moses and the call of God to Joshua. There is a great deal behind the scenes in this part of the story. Moses had died in the fullness of his strength (Deuteronomy 34:7), so that up to the moment of his death he was the one, the only one, who had guided Israel. Even in his increasing age, he had never needed outside assistance—"his eyes were not dim nor his natural vigor abated." Joshua had been Moses' servant. For forty years he had waited on Moses, caring for him and faithfully carrying out all his instructions. In one sense, Joshua had never had to make a decision—Moses spoke and Joshua obeyed. Then suddenly Moses was dead. No more would he give the orders. It was now up to Joshua, who had never made a decision for forty years.

Joshua's reaction was one of immediate fear—not that he was a coward, but the weight of responsibility suddenly became very real and heavy. This is shown in the succeeding verses where God calls to him repeatedly not to be afraid. Added to this responsibility was Joshua's knowledge of the children of Israel. The Bible records many instances where the children of Israel spoke against Moses, murmured against him, and caused him much sorrow of heart by their unreasonable behavior. Joshua was the only man who really knew the extent of the suffering Moses endured at the hands of this rebellious people—and now God was calling *him* to take the place of Moses. He would have not only the decisions to make, but the burdens to bear, and the opposition to face. He would be very conscious of his weakness, of his fear and his complete inability to cope with such a situation. It was to this man, with all his need, that God came presenting His program for victory. The words that God brought to Joshua are for all time and for all people in need. We can take these plans of God and apply them to our own lives as God's basic training plan for successful service.

Verse 3 contains a precious hidden promise: "Every place that the sole of your foot will tread upon I have given to you, as I said to Moses." Notice that God did not mention the sole of your shoe, but *the sole of your foot*. These are two different things. The first time Moses met God (Exodus 3), he had drawn near to a burning bush. He had been commanded to remove his shoes, for the place on which he was standing was holy ground. As Moses stood there with the sole of his foot upon the holy ground, he was both recognizing and demonstrating the presence of God. In other words, the bare foot upon the ground was a sign of the recognition of the presence of God. That was how God guaranteed ultimate victory to Joshua. Every place where Joshua went, if the sole of his foot, not his shoe, was on the ground, then he was recognizing the presence of Almighty God—and the presence of God was an assurance of victory.

Notice the tenses of the verbs in this verse: "Every place that the sole of your foot will tread upon"—future tense—"I have given to you"—past tense. The success of Joshua's faith was already guaranteed. What was to be a future experience with Joshua was already a past certainty with God. And the guarantee was "as I said to Moses." God's fulfilled promises to Moses were the assurance that God would do the same for Joshua in every place.

In verse 5 God promised specific help to Joshua in these words: "No man shall be able to stand before you all the days of your life." Joshua was a young man when they left Egypt (Exodus 33:11), and he had been forty years in the wilderness, so that by the time God brought to him this commission he would be nearly sixty years old. In our day he would have been preparing for retirement. But notice the emphasis of God: "all the days of your life." There was an assurance of many years' service ahead. God backed this up by adding—"as I was with Moses, so I will be with you. I will not leave you nor forsake you." Joshua would remember that Moses was eighty years old when he began his life's work, and that he served God for forty years.

In these days when there is such an emphasis on the importance of youth, it is good to remember that God sometimes chose young men such as Joseph and David or the apostles, but often He used older men such as Moses and Joshua. The thing to realize is that physical age is not the most important factor in Christian service. The one essential is the presence of God. When it comes to growing spiritual muscles, once again physical age is not the deciding factor. There are many mighty "old" men in God's army today, just as there are many weak "young" men.

We have already considered the natural fear that must have filled the heart of Joshua. God answered it in His repeated call: "Be strong and of good courage" (verse 6); "Only be strong and very courageous" (verse 7); "Have I not commanded you? Be strong and of good courage; do not be afraid, nor be dismayed" (verse 9). It is almost as if it took the command of God to guarantee the response of Joshua. This is no reflection on his personal courage. He was strong and brave within his own limitations—but here was a situation that he knew was too big for the resources he possessed, and so automatically he would be fearful and apprehensive about the consequences.

The thing to realize is that physical age is not the most important factor in Christian service. The one essential is the presence of God.

In verse 9 the Lord commanded Joshua to be strong and not to be afraid, and then He added the one phrase that made all things possible: "for the Lord your God is with you wherever you go." Joshua was going to be strong in the strength of another. It is good to realize what it was God actually did for Joshua. There was to be no lessening of the pressure, things were never going to be easier, every problem and difficulty was sure and certain. But what God did was to increase Joshua's resources to meet those problems. A situation only becomes a problem when I do not have sufficient resources to meet it. If I have sufficient resources, then it becomes an incident. This was the great lesson God was teaching Joshua, and it is God's great lesson for us today. The whole business of developing spiritual muscles is linked with the resources from which I operate.

God said to Joshua, "The Lord your God is with you wherever you go"—be strong in the strength of another. The Lord Jesus says to all His followers, "All authority has been given to Me in heaven and on earth. . . . and lo, I am with you always, even to the end of the age" (Matthew 28:18,20). The Amplified Bible presents Hebrews 13:5 most effectively and dramatically:

". . . for He [God] Himself has said, I will not in any way fail you *nor* give you up *nor* leave you without support. [I will] not, [I will] not, [I will] not in any degree leave you helpless, *nor* forsake *nor* let [you] down, (relax My hold on you)! [Assuredly not!]"

A situation only becomes a problem when I do not have sufficient resources to meet it. If I have sufficient resources, then it becomes an incident.

Joshua knew God as an experience outside his own personality. But every child of God who is living in the good of his Christian faith knows a Savior who lives in his heart. So that, in one sense, we are better equipped today to win the battle than Joshua was. But Joshua's great success was that he acted on what God promised him. He continued to draw on his new resources, and as long as he did, he experienced victory.

This fact is underlined in the incident recorded in Joshua 5:13-15. Here Joshua was facing up to his first battle, the attack on the city of Jericho. He was alone, contemplating the city and the situation. Suddenly, "he lifted his eyes and looked, and behold, a man stood opposite him with his sword drawn in his hand" (verse 13). Joshua's immediate reaction was to challenge the newcomer as to which side he was on: "Are you for us, or for our adversaries?" The glory of this story is what followed this challenge: "So He said, 'No, but as Commander of the army of the Lord I have now come.'" Joshua's immediate response was to fall on his face and worship. He asked for orders and the Lord's captain replied, "Take your sandal off your foot, for the place where you stand is holy." This is most significant because no angelic being ever accepted worship. The only inference is that this Captain was divine, that in some wonderful way He was the Lord Jesus manifest in flesh before He took unto Himself the nature of man. This incident would reestablish in Joshua's mind the words God had previously spoken to him: ". . . every place that the sole of your foot will tread upon" (1:3). It would also take him back to the effectual call of Moses recorded in Exodus 3:1-5. There it was a burning bush, here it was a man with a drawn sword—but in both cases it was the voice of God calling, "take your sandal off your foot, for the place where you stand is holy ground."

The whole point was that Joshua, who had been reviewing the Jericho situation with regard to himself and his own capabilities, suddenly realized that his resources were nothing less than God Himself. Nothing could stop him then. The infinite power and provision of the Trinity were the sources upon which he could draw. The God who had brought him out of Egypt was still capable of bringing him into the land of Canaan.

This, too, is the measure of our resources. The Lord Jesus lives in our hearts to be our strength and our power. He who died on the cross to deliver me from the Egypt of my sin and bondage is still doing His gracious work of delivering. He lives in my heart to be the Captain of the host of the Lord in my daily experience. I, too, will be strong in the strength of another. Like Paul in Philippians 4:13 I can say, "I can do all things through Christ who strengthens me." We are not told whether Joshua ever saw the Lord's captain again. In any case, he had no need to. His faith would make real what God had promised, and so victory was his.

God's blueprint for victory detailed in Joshua 1:1-9 had one more essential truth for Joshua to accept. Verse 8 ends with these words "for then you will make your way prosperous, and then you will have good success." Here was the very thing Joshua craved—a prosperous way with good success. But notice the special teaching God put forth in verse 8: "This Book of the Law shall not depart from your mouth; but you shall meditate in it day and night." The book of the law was as much as they had of God's Holy Word in those days. This was Joshua's Bible. He had to meditate on the law day and night—morning and evening Bible study. Remember that Joshua was probably one of the busiest men who ever lived. He was responsible for the total welfare of over two million people—feeding them, supplying water, arranging for disposal of waste products, planning the movement of all these people, settling their differences, and leading their worship. But, in spite of all this time-consuming activity, he was still expected to meditate day and night on the Word of God.

Notice that Joshua was told to *meditate* on the Word of God, not merely to read it. There is a great difference between reading and meditating. Reading is just one-way traffic. My eyes go to the book and move along its lines and pages just reading and recognizing the letters and words. But when I am meditating, I am engaged in two-way traffic. My eyes go to the book and the book comes to me. The information I read there comes to lodge in my mind and in my heart. "Your word I have hidden in my heart, that I might not sin against you" (Psalm 119:11). This is another of the secrets of growing spiritual muscles. Storing the Word of God in the heart helps to provide the resources of strength for daily living. But the most important thing to see in this verse is that meditation in itself is not sufficient to make one's way prosperous, and so to have good success. There is a line of thinking which somehow assumes that if I have read my Bible for the day, then all will be well. Some Christians associate Bible reading with a "luck-charm" experience—if I've read my little bit, then I have guaranteed my safety and blessing all the day.

No, what God said was, ". . . you shall meditate in it day and night, that you may observe to do according to all that is written in it. For then you will make your way prosperous, and then you will have good success."

Only one thing guarantees success: obedience to the Word of God. As I meditate, the Word comes to lodge in my heart and mind. Then the Word within my mind and heart starts to speak to me, to convict me of sins of thought and deed, to show me how I ought to behave in such a situation, and what my actions and reactions should be. My response to the inward working of the Word of God is the measure of my success in God's sight. This was true for Joshua, but it is more important to us today, because we have the Word of God in its entirety. The Bible gives us the complete known, written, and revealed will of God. Our behavior is our response to that revelation. Some will choose to ignore its teaching, claiming it is irrelevant for today. But the thing to remember is that God's basic truth is relevant for all ages.

Only one thing guarantees success: obedience to the Word of God. My response to the inward working of the Word of God is the measure of my success in God's sight.

See, now, how this all lines up with the Word in 1 John 2:14 concerning the young men: "you are strong, and the word of God abides in you, and you have overcome the wicked one." Joshua was going to be strong in the strength of another—and so can we. Joshua was going to meditate on God's Word, and through obedience to the abiding Word he was going to have success and prosperity—and so can we. Joshua was going to overcome the enemy with Christ as the Captain of the Lord's host—and so can we. Just as Joshua acquired spiritual muscles through God's plan for successful leadership, so we can respond in the same way. Using the limitless resources of Christ, we too can turn problems into incidents.

The third group mentioned in 1 John 2:12-14 is "fathers." First it was *little children,* then *young men*, and now *fathers*. We need to remember that if the correct progression is followed, the little children become the young men, and the young men become the fathers. The young men retain the twofold knowledge of the little children—a knowledge of sins forgiven and of the Heavenly Father. Likewise, the fathers retain the three-fold attributes of the young men—"You are strong, and the word of God abides in you, and you have overcome the wicked one," as well as the twofold knowledge of the little children.

An examination of this passage in 1 John shows that there is only one special thing said about the fathers: "you have known Him who is from the beginning" (verses 12 and 14). After learning the other truths, the fathers learn something new. Knowing the One who is from the beginning is a deeper experience which takes them into the counsels of the Godhead. They learn not only *what* God has done, but *why* He did it. Their roots go deep into the eternal truths of God. They are living by Paul's directions in Colossians 2:6: "As you have therefore received Christ Jesus the Lord, so walk in Him." As they continue to walk in this way, the next verse becomes part of their daily experience: "Rooted and built up in Him and established in the faith, as you have been taught, abounding in it with thanksgiving."

The word "fathers" indicates that they have had children and that they are capable of bringing up a family. This also has its spiritual application. Spiritual "fathers" will have led others to Christ; they will have spiritual children, grandchildren, and beyond that. They will also be capable of raising a family, of exercising discipline, of taking on responsibility. These are the kind of Christians who are the choice fruit of the Christian faith. We see them as pastors, missionaries, teachers, church officers, and in a host of other capacities where the faith is abounding through their dedicated lives.

This is how it ought to be—a demonstration of spiritual maturity in the lives of men and women and young people. This is what the world is longing to see—a faith that works. This is what Christ is longing to see, He "who for the joy that was set before Him endured the cross, despising the shame (Hebrews 12:2)."

All this is possible to those who are prepared to spend time developing spiritual muscles through obedience to the Word of God. Age and sex are no barrier; all that is required is a willing, obedient heart.

12

The Secret Of Successful Service

Sometime ago I was reading an article in a missionary magazine which gave statistics on missionary training. I was surprised to see how many missionaries remained at home after their first period of service. There were some who returned home even *before* the end of their first period. I thought of the large investment of time and money which in a sense was wasted, and I wondered why these people went out in the first place. I know there are some who return home ill or physically incapacitated for further service abroad, and it is right and proper that they should stay at home. But when some of the other cases are known and examined, it becomes obvious that they should never have stepped out into missionary training and overseas service. It is obvious that it was not the will of God that some of them should have taken this step.

There are several reasons why people make the mistake of thinking God wants them on the mission field, but there is one factor common to all—an over-emphasized sense of emotional enthusiasm. I have been to missionary meetings where graphic accounts were presented showing the terrible need for people to go and tell of the love of Jesus. Stories were told which moved the hearers to tears. Challenges were presented that were impossible to resist. As the meetings continued, the enthusiasm of the listeners increased. They became emotionally involved in the need that they saw. Then, finally, when an appeal was made calling upon all who were willing to go, I have seen many young people step out into the aisles and walk forward. They did so with eyes aglow, and a glorious sense of adventure for Christ. They were deeply moved and filled with tremendous emotional enthusiasm. And at the time, they really meant business.

All this is good, up to a point. There is a need for enthusiasm, and an emotional involvement in one's task is absolutely necessary. But by themselves, these are not enough. If the call is not from God, then it is a response from the flesh—a flesh that is sincere and willing and loving, but still flesh—and that which is of the flesh cannot please God!

I have seen the joy in the hearts of older members of a church as they have watched these young people going forward in response to such an appeal. They have felt their prayers were being answered, and that soon there would be more people from their church on the mission field. But sometimes this leads to undue pressure being brought on the young people. I remember one boy saying to me that, as the months went by after his response to such a call, people began to hint that he should be stepping out for training. He began to develop a sense of guilt in that he wasn't fulfilling the stand he had made. As the time went by, he and others were subjected to a form of spiritual blackmail. The final result was that some went in for missionary training and went to the mission field overseas. But the thing was not of God, and long before their first period was up they had lost their enthusiasm and their desire to continue. Thus it was that money was wasted, lives were frustrated, and God's work was neglected.

There are some very pointed words about this situation in Ecclesiastes 5:1-7. The first verse of this passage talks about *the sacrifice of fools.* "Walk prudently when you go to the house of God; and draw near to hear rather than to give the sacrifice of fools, for they do not know that they do evil." Several words in the original Hebrew are translated by the one word *fool.* These words have different shades of meaning, such as evil one, boaster, empty person, thickheaded, thoughtless, unwise, heedless, or rebel. The actual meaning of the word for *fool* which is used here is "self-confident." There is no reflection cast on the person's mental capacity or their moral behavior. The picture is rather of a sure sense of absolute self-confidence, a definite putting forward of the flesh, of what self can do. This is borne out by the rest of the passage:

"Do not be rash with your mouth, and let not your heart utter anything hastily before God. . . . It is better not to vow than to vow and not pay. Do not let your mouth to cause your flesh to sin. . ." (verses 2, 5, 6).

Here is a person who is profoundly emotionally moved. At the height of this experience, he makes special vows to God, even in the house of God. But after the heat of the excitement has died down, he goes back on what he has promised. As a result, the mouth causes the flesh to sin.

It is possible to react to God in just the same way today. In one sense, such a response to God can be sin. Romans 14:23 says that "whatever is not from faith is sin." Any action taken only because of emotional enthusiasm is certainly not of faith; it is the energy of the flesh, the *sacrifice of fools*.

There is another form of service mentioned in the Old Testament which we could think of as the "sacrifice of love." Psalm 40 begins by telling of the goodness of God in salvation. David says in verse 5:

"Many, O Lord my God, are Your wonderful works which you have done; and Your thoughts toward us cannot be recounted to You in order; if I would declare and speak of them, they are more than can be numbered."

Any action taken only because of emotional enthusiam is certainly not of faith; it is the energy of the flesh, the sacrifice of fools.

His response to the overwhelming love of God is: "Sacrifice and offering You did not desire; my ears You have opened; burnt offering and sin offering You did not require (verse 6)."

Verse 6 is both unusual and, at first glance, misleading. David has just expressed his great debt to God, but now he appears to say that he is not going to offer any sacrifice of thanksgiving in return. The phrase, "my ears You have opened" seems completely out of place. But it is this short phrase which contains the secret of the sacrifice of love. The Hebrew word translated here as "opened" is really the word "pierced." Verse 6 is saying that there will be no sacrifice and offering because "my ear You have pierced."

The reference is to Deuteronomy 15, which begins with these words: "At the end of every seven years you shall grant a release." It then goes on to describe how debts had to be forgiven in the year of release and all things put right. If any man owned a Hebrew man or woman as a slave, at the end of seven years he had to set him free. ". . . and when you send him away free from you, you shall not let him go away empty-handed; you shall supply him liberally from your flock, from your threshing floor, and from your winepress" (verses 13-14). The slave was to be set free with rich gifts of cattle and wheat and wine.

But then the account goes on to visualize the situation where such a slave might not want to be set free. He is so happy with his master and so contented with his life that he just doesn't want to be set free to care for himself. "If it happens that he says to you, 'I will not go away from you,' because he loves you and your house, since he prospers with you" (verse 16), then the Law of God directed that a strange and unusual ceremony was to take place. The master had to take his slave, either man or woman, and bring him or her to the door of his home. "Then you shall take an awl, and thrust it through his ear to the door, and he shall be your servant forever."

By a definite act of will, this slave became a slave forever. There was no going back, no changing of the mind. Once the ear was pierced, the slave gave up all rights to his own life. No one forced him to have his ear pierced. He did so knowing that from that moment forward he would own absolutely nothing. He made a commitment which was complete. There was nothing left to do, nothing more to give.

So in Psalm 40:6, David said he would make no sacrifice or offering because there was nothing left to sacrifice. He had made a once-for-all decision which needed no repetition. He had become God's slave.

Romans 12:1-2 deals with a similar type of dedication to God: "I beseech you therefore, brethren, by the mercies of God, that you present your bodies a living sacrifice, holy, acceptable to God, which is your reasonable service."

Here is a call to a once-for-all dedication to God. Just as the slave had the pierced ear, so we are called upon to make our *reasonable service*—the presenting of our bodies. Having made this once-for-all act of yielding to God, we have no more sacrifice to give, no more offering to present, no more altar calls to answer. This commitment is complete.

There is only one true response to the pierced hands of Christ—the pierced ear of complete dedication.

That is the way the Bible looks at dedication to Christ, but many churches do not follow this pattern. In some places, there are repeated calls to dedication— my money, my time, my love, my future, etc.—as if I am dedicating small portions of myself and my posses- sions at a time. There is only one true response to the pierced hands of Christ—the pierced ear of complete dedication. Having made this humble and definite once-for-all decision, I can then go forward knowing that *I am not my own.* I don't have to decide for the mission field—I have no more decisions to make. As I walk in unbroken fellowship with my Lord, then I will hear His voice; and as I hear, so I obey. This, then, is the first part of the *secret of successful service*—the plan which God has ordained.

In addition to the plan God has ordained, there is now the pattern which Christ has proclaimed. We can find this pattern set forth in John 17:18 where the Lord Jesus prayed, "As You sent Me into the world, I also have sent them into the world." The risen Christ repeated this thought in John 20:21—"Peace to you! As the Father has sent Me, I also send you." The setting forth of the pattern of service is quite definite—*as . . . so.* *"As my Father has sent Me, so send I you."* The service rendered by the Lord Jesus was complete and perfect in every way, as He Himself said in John 8:29: "I always do those things that please Him." Matthew 3:17 records the words of the Father: "This is My beloved Son, in whom I am well pleased."

The first thing to notice in this pattern of service is that I don't go—I am sent. Christ's words are, "As the Father has sent Me, I also send you." This is most important, because right at the beginning it settles once and for all the motive and the means of my service. If I *go*, then the load is on me; it is *my* plan and *my* responsibility. But if I am sent, then another is responsible for my going, for my plans and preparation.

The pattern is shown quite clearly in Isaiah chapter six. The chapter opens with the young man Isaiah having his great vision of the holiness of God. As a result, he has a sense of his own uncleanness and unworthiness (verse 5). Verses 6 and 7 deal with the cleansing he received. Then in verse 8 came this great call from God: "Also I heard the voice of the Lord, saying, 'Whom shall I send, and who will go for Us?' Then I said, 'Here am I! Send me.'" God was going to do the sending; Isaiah's part was to go. God thus became totally responsible for the mission and service of Isaiah, for God had said "who will go for *Us*"—the Trinity.

Isaiah was responsible for one thing only—to be faithful and available to the Lord who had sent him.

The rest of this chapter gives the conversation between the Lord and Isaiah. Isaiah is told to "go, and tell this people; 'Keep on hearing, but do not understand; keep on seeing, but do not perceive.'" In one sense, Isaiah commenced his service with the promise of failure. He was going to speak, but no one would understand him. He was going to describe the visions, but no one was going to comprehend his message. God prepared Isaiah for this. But since Isaiah was not responsible for making up the messages, he was not responsible for the consequences. If it had been his own ministry, he might have tried new approaches, different techniques, and more attractive presentations. But he wasn't "going;" he was "being sent." Isaiah was to be responsible for one thing only—to be faithful and available to the Lord who had sent him.

1 Corinthians 4:2 gives us this ruling: "Moreover it is required in stewards that one be found faithful"—not necessarily fruitful. The Lord Jesus in Matthew 25:21,23 gave us the same requirement in the story of

the householder who traveled into a far country, leaving his servants to do business for him. On his return the lord said to the servants, "Well done, good and faithful servant."

This same idea is seen in Acts 9 where Saul of Tarsus met the risen Lord on the Damascus road. In verse 6 we read, "So he, trembling and astonished said, 'Lord, what do you want me to do?'" Here was Paul at the commencement of his great service for God asking for directions. The answer to Saul comes in verse 16: "For I will show him how many things he must suffer for My name's sake." Here also was the program and plan for his life—suffering! Humanly speaking, such an idea is unreasonable—a program of suffering! But Paul wasn't "going;" he was "being sent." Isaiah was sent to fail, and Paul was sent to suffer; but both of these servants were faithful and available to the end. All this is part of the secret of successful service.

The second thing to notice is that true service is based on the pattern set by the Lord Jesus. He said, "As the Father has sent me, I also send you." The thought here is *"as . . . so."* The Lord Jesus is going to send me in the same way that He was sent. If I examine the pattern and plan of *His* service, then I will begin to learn the basis upon which *I* will operate. I will find that I will be sent for the same *purpose* Christ was sent. I will be sent in the same *manner* that He was sent, and I will be sent under the same *conditions*. All this will be part of the *as* and *so* of my service.

If we examine the Word of God to find the purpose for the sending of Christ, we will discover many important verses. The Lord Jesus said of Himself, "for the Son of Man has come to seek and to save that which was lost" (Luke 19:10). In John 10:10 He said,

"I have come that they may have life, and that they may have it more abundantly." These and other precious verses give us glimpses of the motives behind the sending of our Lord, but they do not tell us the main purpose for His coming.

John 17 is the prayer of Christ to His Father. It is full of intimacies between the Father and the Son. Verse 4 is a most wonderful declaration, "I have glorified You on the earth. I have finished the work which You gave Me to do." In these words we see the real purpose of the coming of Christ: He came to glorify the Father. He did this in many ways, but everything was with one end in view—to glorify the Father. No one before had ever truly glorified God in thought and word and deed, but here was One who could say, "I always do those things that please Him" (John 8:29). When the Babe was born in Bethlehem, ". . . suddenly there was with the angel a multitude of the heavenly host praising God and saying: 'Glory to God in the highest, and on earth peace, good will toward men!'" The very *coming* of the Babe was glory to God.

If we can bring our hearts to realize that the secret of successful service is to be sent for the same purpose as the Lord Jesus was—to bring glory to God in our every thought and word and deed—then we can reorient many of our ideas. We can draw up a new standard of values and prepare a new order of priorities.

We are not sent primarily to be missionaries, pastors, teachers, or any other kind of worker. There are pastors and teachers who feel that because of the office they hold they are serving God, but who in their daily lives bring no glory to God. There are missionaries whose lives do not glorify God. It isn't the office I hold that signifies my service, but the way in which my Heavenly Father is glorified in the common things of my life. There are little "nobodies" scattered around this world whose lives radiate and glorify God, whose daily doings bring joy to the angels of heaven—and yet in the eyes of this world they are still nobodies!

It isn't the office I hold that signifies my service, but the way in which my Heavenly Father is glorified in the common things of my life.

This business of bringing glory to God is for all to engage in, young and old, rich and poor, educated and ignorant. This is why down through the ages God has never been short of praise and glory and honor, because there are always those whose love is so earnest that the glory just flows. Mark 12:37 is always true: "and the common people heard him gladly." When the rest of my service is geared to this one thrust of glorifying God, then all service becomes infinitely precious and valuable, and even the ordinary things take on a new sense of wonder.

Another secret of successful service is to learn that we are sent, not only for the same purpose, but also in the same manner as the Lord Jesus: *"As the Father has sent me, I also send you."* The Lord Jesus expressed some very deep truths in His discourse recorded in John 6:26-71. Verse 57 comes as a great challenge to our hearts: "as the living Father sent Me, and I live because of the Father, so he who feeds on Me will live because of Me." Here the Lord Jesus taught that the living Father had sent Him and He lived by the Father. He, the Son, is now sending us and as we eat of Him, Christ, so we shall live by Him. This type of teaching was misunderstood by many of His disciples. The Amplified Bible puts it this way:

"When His disciples heard this, many of them said, This is a hard *and* difficult *and* strange saying (an offensive and unbearable message). Who can stand to hear it? [Who can be expected to listen to such teaching?]" Verse 66 says, "From that time many of his disciples went back and walked with Him no more."

The tragedy is that today men still go back and walk no more with Jesus. This is basic teaching regarding successful service, and it needs to be faced up to and grasped. The Lord said, "he who feeds on Me will live because of Me." How can I eat Him? Verse 63 is a help in this matter: "It is the Spirit who gives life; the flesh profits nothing. The words that I speak to you are spirit, and they are life." In other words, the explanation is completely spiritual, although the illustration is physical.

The ordinary food that I eat day by day makes me what I am physically. I become what I eat. If I eat good food and have a well-balanced diet, I will be as physically fit as possible. If I eat poor food, my strength will suffer. If I eat diseased food, I will be ill. If I eat poisoned food, I will die. This is an obvious fact. But the same thing applies to the rest of my human personality. I have a soul or heart as well as a body. My soul is composed of my mind, my emotions, and my will. These I also feed daily, and the food they receive decides the health of my soul. If I feed my soul the trash of the world in literature, art, music, radio, and television, then I must not be surprised if my soul is sick and powerless to face the burdens and temptations of daily life. But if I allow the Lord Jesus to move within my mind, my emotions, and my will, then my soul's health will be braced and full of vitality. *"He who feeds on me will live because of me."* As I feed on Christ in thought and word and deed, then I become like Him. There will be a purity, a peace, and a quiet joy which will be all of Him. I will be morally, mentally, and spiritually equipped to be sent "in the same manner." I will have a strength and a peace which are not my own.

I feed on Christ as His word is hidden in my heart. "Your word I have hidden in my heart, that I might not sin against You" (Psalm 119:11). I seek His will for my will and am willing to obey it at all costs. My emotions are the vehicle of His love and compassion. My mind is the ever-ready, ever-available means for His purposes to be worked out. This is a gradual process, part of the spiritual machinery of growing in grace. There is no alternative to feeding on Christ, if I want my service to be marked with Christlike qualities and to be followed by Christlike success.

The disciples in the story in John 6 were quite happy to be occupied with Christ, to be where He was and to listen to His teaching. But the Lord Jesus asked for more than occupation; He wanted *identification* with Himself. He wanted men who would be involved with Him, men into whose lives He could move and operate in depth.

Another secret of successful service is to learn that we are sent, not only for the same purpose and in the same manner as Jesus Christ, but under the same conditions. These thoughts we have already considered in a previous chapter, but it is also essential to see this truth with regard to successful service.

When we consider the verse, "As the Father has sent Me, I also send you," it seems in one way to be asking too much of us. We realize that the Lord Jesus was the Son of God, that He was deity, that, "All things were made through Him, and without Him nothing was made that was made" (John 1:3). Then we ask ourselves, "How can we be expected to serve in the same way as the Son of God? He had all the power. He could raise the dead, still the storm, change water into wine. Surely it is impossible for us to be sent under the same conditions."

This might be the reasoning of our hearts until we consider the verses which show us the "nothingness" of Christ. John's gospel contains that series of statements from the lips of Christ in which He claims no personal authority for His deed, His will, His teaching or His words.

John 5:19—"The Son can do nothing of Himself."

John 5:30—"I can of myself do nothing . . . because I do not seek My own will but the will of the Father who has sent Me."

John 7:16—"My doctrine is not Mine, but His who sent Me."

John 8:28, 29—"I do nothing of Myself; . . . He who sent Me is with Me."

John 14:10—"The words that I speak to you, I do not speak on My own authority; but the Father who dwells in Me does the works."

When it came to service, the Lord Jesus was entirely and utterly dependent on the Father who had sent Him. He claimed the presence of the Father dwelling within Him, and He placed Himself unreservedly at the disposal of the Father. He could say in John 4:34, "My food is to do the will of Him who sent Me, and to finish His work." We find that it was not His *deity* that made the service successful, but His *dependence* on the One who sent Him.

This then is the third secret of successful service in our lives. The Lord Jesus said, "As the Father has sent me, I also send you"—under the same conditions, to be absolutely dependent on the One who sends us. It will be our joy to say with Jesus, "He who sent Me is with Me." Claiming His presence, and utterly dependent on His purpose and power, we can go on to experience a quality of service which is patterned on that of the Son of God Himself.

13

The Secret Of Constant Fruitfulness

Genesis 1:28 contains the first recorded words of God to the man and woman He had created. "Then God blessed them, and God said to them, 'Be fruitful and multiply; fill the earth and subdue it; have dominion. . . .'" God gave to Adam and Eve a threefold instruction—to produce, to replenish, and to reign. The first command was to be fruitful (to reproduce). When we look around today at any living things, whether they are animals or fishes, insects or flowers, vegetables or trees, the one driving force common to every living form is *life reproducing itself.* The rose is not growing sweet flowers for the pleasure of mankind; it is seeking to reproduce itself. The main purpose behind the vast complex order of parents and offspring is simply reproduction. Whatever God has created or ordained is working under this same relentless impulse to multiply and reproduce.

John 15:16 records some striking words spoken by the Lord Jesus: "You did not choose Me, but I chose you and appointed you that you should go and bear fruit, and that your fruit should remain." Here we find the Lord Jesus giving the purpose of our Christian experience. We did not choose Him; He chose us. And

He chose us for a special purpose, that we should bear fruit—fruit that would remain.

The first time we were born, we received physical life. But when we were born again as Christians, we received another kind of life through the indwelling presence of the Holy Spirit of Christ. Just as physical

---

A church that fails to reproduce its "life" soon withers and becomes a social organization instead of a living organism.

---

life continues and fulfills its purpose in every form by being fruitful and reproducing, so it is with spiritual life. A spiritual life which is not seeking with great earnestness to reproduce itself is a life completely out of touch with the purposes of God. The energies of such a life, if there are any, are all misdirected; the power, if there is any, is wasted on less important purposes. A species that fails to reproduce soon becomes extinct. A church that fails to reproduce its "life" soon withers and becomes a social organization instead of a living organism. A Christian who is not fruitful for God is a spiritual monstrosity, something outside the order of true creation.

So it is that this final chapter is the most vital chapter of the book. It deals with the questions of real fruitfulness—*the secret of constant fruitfulness.* Apart from such a constant experience, I cannot justify my existence in the sight of God. Much of the real tragedy of the Christian world today is that we have thousands upon thousands of Christians who are busily intent

upon being successful, grateful, worshipful, enthusiastic, moral, respectable—and missing the first and
foremost command of all—*be fruitful*. Nothing
continues unless it reproduces itself, because this is
God's way of maintaining life.

The discourse recorded in John 15 was given at a
crucial time in the life of Christ. Behind Him lay His
ministry, before Him stood the cross. Before He
moved into the final drama of redemption, He gave
these words of vital importance. Christ was the
heavenly "grain of wheat" that was about to fall into
the ground and die, so that He could bring forth much
fruit (John 12:24). In this chapter He gave His
greatest teaching on the secret of the believer's life of
fruitfulness. He who was about to initiate a grain of
everlasting fruitfulness gave all the instructions we
would need so that we, even in our day and generation, could follow in His steps and bring forth fruit
that would remain.

It is interesting to note what Christ chose as the
symbol of fruitfulness, and why He chose it. He spoke
of Himself as the true vine and His disciples as the
branches. I can still remember how amazed I was when
I first understood the full meaning of this illustration.
My only connection with an actual vine was what I
knew of the great vine at Hampton Court, in London,
England. This vine is a tremendous thing enclosed in
a huge greenhouse, almost like a vast museum
specimen in a glass case. It is hundreds of years old
and has roots which are supposed to reach down to the
River Thames. It is called "The Father of All Vines"
and has been bearing hundreds of bunches of grapes
down through the years.

Several years ago, however, when I was being driven from Los Angeles out to Forest Home Conference Center, my education concerning vines was improved and extended. As we journeyed along the freeway, I saw a large notice which informed me that we were approaching the world's largest vineyard. Apparently the vineyard extended out on both sides of the freeway. But when I looked for the vines as I expected to see them, there was nothing to be seen or recognized. I asked the driver where the vines were, and he told me I was looking at them. So I stared more intently and finally asked him if those endless rows of sticks were the vines—such miserable little things they were! The branches were so twisted they appeared to be suffering from a permanent form of rheumatoid arthritis. They had no beauty either in shape or foliage.

Since that day I have learned that the flowers of a vine are unimpressive, that the wood of the vine is useless as timber, and that even the broken branches are of little use for making a good, steady fire because they flare up suddenly and are burned out in no time. In many ways, the vine is a useless plant— except for the one tremendous fact that it bears grapes. Apart from its possible fruitfulness, the vine is useless to man!

How strange that the Lord Jesus should choose the branches of a vine to represent our relation to Himself, and yet how true it is in every respect. There is no beauty in us. There is nothing in us that could possibly make us attractive to God. The Bible uses one special word to describe all that a man is without Christ—the word *flesh*. All the glory of the natural man—all his potential, abilities, dynamic outreach—is summed up and contained in the one word *flesh*. "So then, those who are in the flesh cannot please God" (Romans 8:8). There is absolutely nothing in the natural fallen man to make him useful or acceptable to God. He is no more valuable than a broken-off branch.

By using the figure of the branches and the vine, the Lord Jesus taught the one basic lesson about fruitfulness which so many Christians miss completely. In all His references to fruitbearing, the Lord Jesus taught that it isn't the activity of the branches that brings the luscious bunches of grapes. The branches "bear" the fruit—they do not "produce" it.

For years I sought to serve God on the basis of another idea—that *activity* is fruitfulness! I felt that the more enthusiasm I put into my service, the more success I would see. It seemed so simple and so

---

In all His reference to fruitbearing, the Lord Jesus taught that it isn't the activity of the branches that brings the luscious bunches of grapes. The branches "bear" the fruit—they do not "produce" it.

---

logical—the more you worked, the more you produced, and the more you produced, the more fruitful you were. I have met many sincere pastors, missionaries, Sunday school teachers, and other Christian workers whose lives are geared to this same concept—activity is fruitfulness, and enthusiasm ensures success. But it is not so.

This does not imply in the slightest, however, that we should not work hard or that we should dampen our enthusiasm in and for our work. But it does mean exactly what the Lord Jesus said—the branches *bear* the fruit, they don't produce it.

Here is the reason so many sincere Christians reach the point of exhaustion. They work so hard, but never see the fruit they desire. There comes a sense of spiritual frustration which leads on to spiritual fear and guilt. They ask themselves if they have worked hard enough, or if they are keeping anything back that is stopping the blessing. Consequently, they struggle and strive all the more to produce the fruit they yearn for. Soon their life becomes a case of desperate determination which sometimes ends in disaster. The tragedy of a nervous breakdown is often the result of trying with repeated sincerity to produce fruit.

Just suppose, for a moment, that the branches *did* produce the fruit. How different the whole setup would be. The branches would have to struggle and writhe and jerk and thresh until there came the blessed moment when they *squeezed* the grapes out of their branch ends. They would then flop, exhausted by the struggles they had endured. Presently, one branch would look at another and say, "Ha! I've got more grapes than you have!" To which the other would reply, "Maybe! But mine are bigger than yours!" The whole idea is silly and senseless from a vine's point of view, but it is the way many Christians operate in the field of fruitfulness. Producing leads to comparison, and comparison leads to contempt.

What actually happens is that in God's good time, the branches bear blossoms. In God's good time, the blossoms are fertilized and wither. Presently, the withered blossoms reveal tiny things which in God's good time become grapes. All the branch has to do is to be available to cooperate with God, and eventually to bear what God has developed by His own mighty power.

The word the Lord Jesus taught was *abiding*, not *producing*. In John 15:4, He said, "As the branch cannot bear fruit of itself, unless it abides in the vine, neither can you, unless you abide in Me." Notice those

---

The purpose of fruit bearing is not to beautify or glorify the branch. There is one main thrust behind all the fruit bearing—the reproduction of the life of the vine.

---

tremendous words—*neither can you*. When the branch abides in the vine it is doing nothing strange or unusual, but only what God intended branches to do. It is the sap, the life of the vine, which both initiates and maintains the possibility of fruitfulness. The life flows from the roots, up the main stem, and out along the branches. Each branch is fed by the same life, and as long as the branch abides in the vine, knit to the stem with all the divine intricacy of God, the life will flow.

The purpose of the flowing life is to bring about the bearing of fruit. The purpose of fruit bearing is not to beautify or glorify the branch. There is one main thrust behind all the fruit bearing—the reproduction of the life of the vine. Every natural grape contains seeds which possess the secret of life. Each seed, if properly planted and cared for, will result in a new and complete vine. If the *branch* had produced the seed, then the seed would eventually produce only a branch. But because the life of the *vine* produced the seed, then the life of the vine is reproduced in each succeeding generation. The true Christian is one who possesses the life of Christ—the risen Christ is resident in his heart and life. True Christian fruit bearing results in the reproduction of *Christ's* life in the hearts and lives of others.

It is possible for a man to be a great leader, and by his own efforts and dynamic personality to reproduce himself in the lives of others. Thus it was that Hitler was "reproduced" in and through the Nazi Party in Germany. Hitler determined the pattern and the mold, and thousands of Germans reproduced the design in their own lives. The same thing can be dangerously true of an outstanding pastor or Christian worker. The fruit they produce will be the reproduction of their own personality. The branch will be busily reproducing branches, and not vines! And branches are useless, however many there may be, unless they abide in the vine. The Life is the one essential—and Jesus said, "I am the way, the truth, and the life" (John 14:6).

An examination of John chapter 15 shows us that the Lord Jesus also indicated three qualities or degrees of fruitbearing. Verse 2 speaks of *fruit* and *more fruit*. Verses 5 and 8 speak of *much fruit*. So we see that there is a possibility of bearing fruit, of bearing more fruit, and of bearing much fruit.

In verse 1, Jesus says, "I am the true vine, and My Father is the vinedresser." This is important to know, because here we are taught that God is the vinedresser or the gardener. It is *God* who assumes the responsibility for caring for and controlling the vines. Jesus continues in verse 2: "every branch in Me that does not bear fruit He takes away; and every branch that bears fruit He prunes, that it may bear more fruit." Here the Lord Jesus teaches us some of the secrets of the Heavenly Gardener. He said that when a branch is bearing fruit, the Gardener comes and prunes it, that it may bear more fruit. The Gardener is not content with "fruit"; He wants "more fruit." In order to get it, He prunes the branch. Notice that He doesn't prune the vine. He prunes the *branch*—and we are the branches.

Pruning is always a very practical process. It is not a case of words, but of deeds. When a gardener prunes a tree he uses a knife, a pair of secateurs (which are very powerful scissors) and a saw. Pruning is also a "painful" process. Promising young shoots are cut back to two or three buds, and sometimes the very center of the tree is cut out to allow room for expansion. Any sign of disease is treated with the knife or saw, so that the removal of the infected part protects the rest of the tree. And pruning is a planned process, the result of the scheme of the gardener. The tree sends out vigorous shoots in all directions, seeking, as it were, to express its own design for expansion. But when the gardener comes, he imposes his will above the outreach of the tree. Finally, pruning is a limiting process. The tree is always smaller at the end of the operation—not bigger!

I remember what happened when I lived in the south of England. In our garden we had about a hundred apple trees. Most of them, however, were useless as fruit bearing trees. They were large, diseased, and usually had a crop of small, misshapen apples covered with blotches and scabs. If I had had the time, I would have cut them down and burned them. However, close to the house were about a dozen small, really lovely apple trees. They bore apples which were superb in quality and size. When pruning time came, usually in January, I went into my garden armed with my knife, my secateurs, and my saw. I set to work on the lovely, useful trees, employing all my skill and knowledge as a gardener. I cut and clipped and sawed until eventually the trees were to my satisfaction. I planned how this branch should grow in this direction, and that branch in that direction. If necessary, I cut away a whole section of a tree. When I had finished, the trees looked quite different, and all were much smaller. I had a heap of twigs and branches for burning—good twigs and good branches—but I had removed them because they did not fit in with my plans for my trees. I wanted more fruit from these good trees and in order to get it, I pruned them hard. I had one purpose in mind—more fruit!

When the day's work was over and I left the garden, I sometimes imagined what would happen if the trees could talk to each other. I was sure the big useless trees at the end of my garden would look in pity on the twelve small trees, cropped of their shoots and branches. They would say, "My, how that gardener must hate you! He just cuts and saws away at you and removes all those lovely new growths. He doesn't do a thing to us; he just lets us grow any way we wish. It isn't fair. Why should he love us and hate you?" They might think that way, but it wouldn't be true. The fact that nothing happened to them wasn't a proof of my care for them, but of my complete disinterest in them. The fact that the small trees were pruned wasn't a sign of my hatred, but of my love. Pruning isn't punishment. It is the purposeful application of the gardener's plans.

The Lord Jesus said, "my Father is the vinedresser." God is the Gardener who, armed with His knife, secateurs, and saw, prunes the branches of the vine for one purpose only—*that they may bring forth more fruit.* I can look back over my life now and understand why certain things happened in my experience. When these events occurred years ago, they were disappointments, sorrows and, in some cases, tragedies I couldn't begin to understand. I would wonder why God had allowed "this," and why "that" should come into my life. But now I understand—God was pruning, not punishing.

Pruning isn't punishment. It is the purposeful application of the gardener's plans.

He was cutting out vigorous shoots and directing the growth into other directions. I had planned to go into "this" work, but God clipped it out, and the growth was guided into other areas. The most comforting thing is to realize now that God was right. I can now say "Thank You" for what I once resisted. I do not understand all the ways of God, but someday "we shall know as we are known."

It is so satisfying to realize and appreciate that God is the Gardener, that the tools are in His hand, that everything has a purpose, and that all is done in love.

There is "fruit," "more fruit" and "much fruit." It is good to realize, in verse 8, that "by this My Father is glorified, that you bear much fruit." God is only glorified when we bear "much fruit." If "man's chief end is to glorify God and enjoy Him for ever," then this is the only way to do it—to bear much fruit! A comparison between verses 2 and 5 shows us one important difference. Verse 2 speaks of "a branch in Me" bearing fruit; but verse 5 gives an important addition: "He who abides in Me, and I in him, bears much fruit." The extra words *and I in him* are the secret of the "much fruit."

Every true Christian is "in Christ," as 2 Corinthians 5:17 teaches: "Therefore, if anyone is in Christ, he is a new creation." But not every Christian is living in the reality of the fact of the indwelling life of Christ. It is only when there is the *Christ in him* experience that bearing much fruit is possible.

The Lord Jesus added at the end of John 15:5, "for without Me you can do nothing." With these words, *without me,* the Lord Jesus shattered the whole of our human conception of service. Consider the word "nothing." Sometimes when we use the word "nothing" we really mean "not very much." Someone says "Do you have any money with you?" and we answer, "No, nothing." We may actually have a few cents, but "nothing" means "not very much." However, the word "nothing" which the Lord Jesus used is a special word meaning "no thing, not even one." What He actually said was, "for without Me you can do no thing, not even one."

What a challenge this is to our hopes and desires for much fruitful service. It is possible to be in this blessed position only when I have learned the secret of abiding in Christ, and Christ abiding in me. We have thought along these lines in previous chapters of this book, but here the challenge is final and complete. Christ abiding in me, Christ operating through me, Christ using me as the vehicle for His purposes—this is the only way to the fruitfulness of much fruit. The alternative is "no thing, not even one."

It is also essential to remember that the "me" in whom Christ dwells, and through whom He operates, is that trinity of my personality—my mind, my emotions, and my will. The life of the vine must flow through the branch, through every section of the branch. The life of the vine is not only the life of the fruit. It is also the life that feeds the very branch itself. In the actual wooden branch of the vine, what isn't fed by the sap just fails and is withered. Likewise, the spiritual branch that isn't fed just fails. But the branch that is fed is fruitful. As my mind and emotions and will are wide open to the life of Christ, so He is able to cleanse and control, to feed and to make fruitful.

Abiding requires obedience. Abiding *is* obedience—and obedience is something we *learn* as we continue to grow in grace. For this we have Christ's own example. Hebrews 5:8-9 says concerning Him:

"Though He was a Son, yet he learned obedience by the things which He suffered. And having been perfected, He became the author of eternal salvation to all who obey Him."

How amazing to think that the Lord Jesus learned obedience by the things which He suffered! Isaiah 11:1 says concerning Him, "There shall come forth a Rod from the stem of Jesse, and a Branch shall grow out of his roots." This prophecy of the coming Messiah named Him the Branch. As a Branch, He learned obedience through the special pruning of the hand of

God. But what a glorious "much fruit" resulted from His obedience!

Here then is our pattern and our purpose. The secret of constant fruitfulness is first, the obedience of constant abiding; then, a sure understanding of the fact that constant fruit comes from constantly "bearing" the fruit of the vine, and that in no way is the fruit produced by the branch. Finally, we reach our goal when, through the complete sufficiency of the indwelling Christ, we bear much fruit to the constant glory of God the Father.

WITHOUT THEE

John 15:5

"Without Thee"—Lord, Thy promise stands,
That all my work leaves empty hands.
It is Thyself, Thy life in me,
That brings true blessings all can see.

My struggles, tears and wretched strife
Are part and parcel of my life.
There is a peace, a power, a joy,
All waiting now me to employ.

How strange it is, in days gone by,
My Christian life was try and try.
Now, Lord, I've found the secret true,
Thy life in me lived through and through.

'Twas easy then to say the phrase
"God works in many wondrous ways."
But now, 'tis marvelous to see
God works His wonders out through me.

"Greater is He that in you lives"—
How great the promise that He gives.
His risen life, dynamic power,
Are mine to use through every hour.

I simply bring myself and stand
Safe in the hollow of His hand.
Untold delights and joys exist.
In having all I so long missed.

He clothes Himself with such as me,
Puts on my frail humanity;
Then using me to do His will,
He can, in me, His work fulfill.

'Tis His responsibility,
His plan, His peace, His power—not me,
I rest in His abounding grace
And gaze with rapture on His face.

"Without Me—ye can nothing do"
Nothing—not one—Thy word is true.
How terribly we fail to see
Thy word which tells us—"Without Me."

I thought it meant—without Thy Will,
Without Thy help and yet, Lord, still
Thy word stands simple, clear and true—
Not without these—but without You.

Thou art the Truth, the Life, the Way.
"All power belongs to Thee," we say;
How simply, Lord, could we but see
It is not help we need—but Thee.

Then grant me, Lord, the grace to rest,
Quiet, confident, obedient, blest,
Believing all Thy promise true—
I can do all things, Lord—through You.

John Hunter